GOLDEN ECLIPSE:

HEART DOG

A TRUE STORY

Howard W. Schultheis

Copyright © 2013 by Howard W.Schultheis

Table of Contents

This book has a four way dedication

For Wesley H., and Dorothy P. Schultheis who by their actions showed me what loving a dog was all about.

For my wife Ronnie, who would not allow me to, "not get another dog."

For Long Island Golden Retriever Rescue. Simply the best!

And of course for Eclipse, for being Eclipse.

Preface

"A dog is not "almost human," and I know of no greater insult to the canine race than to describe it as such."
- John Holmes

First, I would like to thank you for choosing to read this book. Please don't look for a particular style of writing, mainly because there isn't any. I'm certain that I have made many errors in grammar, sentence structure, tense, chapter organization, etc. If for some strange reason I haven't, it's totally the work of coincidence, with an assist from "spell check." {At the end of January 2014 I corrected my typos. Now you won't find any messtakes. Oh, well.} Any factual errors are mine alone. Along with my wife's help, I tried to remember all the details of many events. Of course there are times when we don't know what we ate for breakfast, so you'll have to excuse us. You see, the intended reader of these pages was originally meant to be only me, as a type of grief therapy, and I certainly wouldn't notice the errors, having been the one that created them.

Another reason I have chosen to share these pages with the world, or the three or four people I beg to purchase it, whichever the case may be, is to raise money for Golden Retriever Rescue. All proceeds from this writing will be donated to Long Island Golden Retriever Rescue.

On August 12th, 2012 we were forced to make a decision. It's one that almost all pet owners have to make, so I'm sure there are many out there who can relate. A sudden life threatening disease had just been discovered, and a choice had to be made between euthanasia and surgery. While this was a decision we had made at other times, and while they were all quite traumatic, they paled in comparison. Any dog we ever had was always given all the love and care my wife and I could shower upon it. This was different. This was Eclipse! As you read these pages you will come to see what I mean by this statement.

Introduction

The beginning chapters of this book contain some information about dogs in my life that I have had. I do not talk about them to demonstrate my canine knowledge, which was just about non-existent. My basic reasoning was to give the reader an idea of where I was "coming from." Each dog was unique, as they always are. One characteristic was constant, however. They were all deeply loved and cared for.

There are chapters in here that were written before other chapters that actually occurred earlier. I felt that where and when I wrote the pages was very important, and had to be taken into account. If the organization causes you any confusion, I apologize.

The bulk of the book tells the amazing, true story, of Eclipse. She was and always will be my, "Heart Dog."

My Definition of a HEART DOG

We love all dogs we have ever had. If you are really lucky there will be that one dog that spiritually and emotionally becomes one with you. Your "hearts," become one. You both seem to know the others emotions, and communicate on a non-verbal level. Somehow you just seem to know what the other's needs are, and you live to take care of them. In a word, the connection is indescribable. If you are lucky enough to someday have a, "Heart Dog, " in your life, you will just know it

Florida Sunshine

"Don't worry about that, there's no way!"

My wife and I were on a short vacation in Florida. We met up with a couple that we had known for many years, and were just sitting around a resort pool and letting the world go by without us. Having worked as elementary school teachers, retirement was new to us, but something easy to get used to. We had loved our jobs, but as most people would tell you, your freedom to just do what you want, when you want is limited. School vacations were obviously the only time we could go away for a few days. Of course trying to get airline tickets, hotel reservations and the like, at reasonable prices was always a challenge, if not an impossibility. Yes, the good life. All of a sudden, little spur of the moment trips on off holiday times were available. You could get up in the morning and decide that it was a great day to just take a ride somewhere, have dinner out, etc., particularly on uncrowded weekdays.

My friend Mike (whom I had taught with for over thirty years) and I, had always had dogs. Unfortunately mine had just passed away. Somehow we got talking about canines, and he made the statement, "Don't get another dog! They are wonderful, but are so dependent on you that you wind up organizing your life around them."

As many dog owners will tell you, any dog you have at the present time is your "LAST DOG." We love them but never want to go through the pain of losing one ever again. As far as tying you down, that is kind of a given. They are family members who can't just be shipped off to stay with grandma while you go on vacation, etc. (Unless you are really lucky and the dog's "grandmutter," and "grandpaw," live close by, and love them as much as you do.) I had made the decision that there would be no more dogs for me, even though I love them. It was the time in my life when travel, carefree days, spontaneous outings etc., were called for. A dog would certainly not fit into the equation, knowing that should I get a new "best friend," I would get too attached and wind up planning my life around him or her. Yes, the decision of no more animals was not discussable. Well, let's put it this way. I knew the topic was not discussable, but apparently no one told my wife.

Canine History

Growing up in Queens, NY, I was an only child. My father was a NYC fireman, while my mother took over the homemaker role with gusto. I really can't remember a time when we didn't have a dog. It was an inconvenience since we lived in an apartment on the second floor of a two family home. Below us, the landlord didn't want to hear any noise from above. It was the mid forties, and my parents always told me that even finding a place that would accept a child was difficult. They had a dog called Skipper, who they said would lay by my crib all day. For some reason I was acceptable to the home owners, but the dog had to go. I recall my parents saying that they cried for days, but had to give up the dog. Looking back I feel real bad about Skipper, but on the other hand I compliment them on their decision to not take one of the many available apartments that would take a dog, but not a child. There was always a chance I could have wound up in a shelter ☺

In my work in golden retriever rescue (more on that later) I talk to people who say things like, "My child is allergic to the dog, " or "Having a baby and a dog in the house at the same time is just too much to handle." These statements result in the dog having to leave. Sometimes I feel the decision as to who should "go" is made without giving it enough thought ☺

My parents were well liked by the landlord, so a dog was finally allowed. I do remember having a cocker spaniel named Sandy, a beagle named Penny, and a German shepherd, Rex, all of whom died young, but the details are fuzzy. Canine medical treatment back in the fifties was just not what it is today.

We moved to our own home just before I entered High School. For a couple years we were dogless. Beats me why, since we all loved animals. Around the time I started college, my father, now a bank appraiser after retiring from the NYC Fire Department, was out looking at a house about forty miles from where we lived. He came home and casually mentioned that the owner had some basset/beagle puppies, who were very cute. Now, my sense of direction at the time was terrible. Maps rarely helped me. Somehow the next day I found the place and immediately fell in love with one of the cute little guys. The next day my father comes home with this little fellow. We named him King. And he was.... king of the house that is.

Certain rules were put in place immediately. Rule one....no dog on the bed. We kept that one for a whole day. From then on I let him share my bed, or should I say he let me sleep with him? We called him my brother, and that's about what it felt like. Always kind of wondered which one of us children was loved the most? Lucky for me, my parents had enough love to go around. When I got married and moved out, about fifty miles away to eastern Long Island, they said the dog stayed with them. I guess they could let me go, but not my brother. I could certainly understand that.

On Our Own

Back in the late sixties my wife and I moved to a part of Long Island that was considered one step short of the wilderness by many. I taught in a small one building school district on the north shore, while she taught in a local district on the south shore. We rented a small home about a half mile from the water near where my wife Ronnie worked. It was an eighteen mile drive, and some days I saw a few other cars. Yes, it was like that out on Long Island at one time.

During my second year of teaching I had the dreaded "cafeteria duty." As a new teacher you did whatever was asked of you with a smile on your face. My custodian friend who worked in the cafeteria saw a dog outside, so out we went to give it something to eat. He said it had been hanging around for a day or so.

I used to be one of the last to leave the building at night. Naturally, who is sitting outside near my car? It's like they have a sensor that can spot a soft touch a mile away. I remember having a 1947 Dodge at the time. I thought I'd take her home for the night and see that she had a good meal and a place to sleep. Well, those were the plans anyway.

I used to pick up my wife at her school on my way home. I parked by the exit door, and hid. Out she comes and what does she see? A dog behind the steering wheel! I guess I should have known that this was a sign of something.

Home we went. The decision to keep the dog took a long time. Probably over thirty minutes as I remember. Our landlord and neighbor had two dogs, both of whom liked our new friend, so all was good. At that point in my life I dug and sold clams to supplement my income, since both my wife and I were going for our masters degrees, with all the associated costs. Our new friend runs out, grabs a chowder clam and runs around with it. We didn't have a name for her yet, so she took matters into her own paws. Chowder was about a one year old shepherd mix. Mixed with what I really couldn't say. Her ears came out straight to the side for a few inches and then bent straight down for a few more. For those of you old enough to remember the television show, "The Flying Nun," with Sally Field, just think of her headpiece. If you are saying things like Sally who?, or a flying what?, you owe it to yourself to check out the old shows. Nothing like them.

The second day we had Chowder we noticed some drops of blood on the floor. No cut pads on her feet, or anything else noticeable, but the blood kept showing up. Yup, she was in heat. The books said this could last a maximum of 28 days. It did. At that time no one had a fenced in yard. Basically dogs ran loose. At the back of the house was a sliding glass door. For a month you would part the curtains by the door to be greeted by an assortment of suitors. Taking Chowder out was obviously a challenge as well. We survived the month without becoming grandparents.

There were no streetlights at that time in our neighborhood. After Labor Day very few cars could be seen around our area. At times Chowder would like to roam. We would take our giant Pontiac Bonneville hardtop (V8, four carbs, dual exhaust that got less than 10 miles to the gallon.....ah, the good old days) and put the windows all down. On a hardtop there is no column between the two side windows. Driving slowly and calling her name usually resulted in her jumping through the open windows. How she knew which car, or could calculate the right path to the window area of a moving vehicle I never will know.

Chowder was always a great dog. She could be totally trusted not to bother anyone. She lived a nice 11 year life, and brought much joy to our lives. I hope we added joy to hers. Finally she was diagnosed with cancer in the nasal area and had to be put to sleep. This was the first time in my life that I had to make this type of decision. Knowing it was the right one doesn't make it much easier. My "brother" King was buried at an animal cemetery and Chowder was laid to rest in the double grave with him. They had always gotten along well, so this seemed appropriate. For anyone who has not seen an animal cemetery you have no idea what it is like. There are regular headstones, sprinkler systems, flowers on many graves, and at Christmas time you will see a great many burial plots and headstones with toys on them, not to mention battery powered Christmas lights (yes, some people do go a bit overboard, but I'm sure it brings them comfort to do these things, and that's really all that matters)

From a Clam to a Volkswagen

Since Chowder was a shepherd mix we decided to get a pure breed German shepherd. I used to take my class each year on a little outing to a local kennel that I used to board Chowder at. They were always very friendly and would let the children hold the puppies. Obviously the perfect place to get our next canine companion. Live and learn.

At the time they had two Shepherds, and we met them in a room one at a time. The first was a larger dog who just wanted to play with you and couldn't settle down. The second was a timid little thing who hid under a chair. My reasoning was simple. It's a whole lot easier to "bring the quiet one out," than to calm the hyper one down. In retrospect, I now understand that my reasoning process was about as reversed as it could get.

They gave us a small container that just about fit the dog and said it was best for training to keep her in there when we weren't home. Again, very sensible sounding at the time, and very stupid looking back. About my only defense is that it was the early eighties and I figured experts knew what they were doing. Not necessarily the case.

We had purchased a home in the early seventies across the street from where we lived with Chowder, and my parents lived next door. We were so excited, and called them over to see our new family member. They entered the back yard and the puppy proceeds to demonstrate growling techniques as well as showing them the size of her teeth. Should have raised a red flag perhaps? We put the dog in the car and went over to the beach where she again goes into her attack dog mode when a couple comes near. It's over thirty years ago, but I still remember the man saying, "You don't have to worry about the silverware with that one." He turned out to be right. We never worried about the silverware, but did have to be concerned with just about everything else!

Her name? We figured that a German shepherd should have a German name. My mother spoke quite a bit of German, and we could have asked her to come up with something, but instead I used my extensive German vocabulary. I had owned a Volkswagen and at one time a Porsche, but neither of those seemed right. Care to guess at her name. Jetta (a type of Volkswagen). Different you must admit. Maybe not on the "Chowder," level but original.

A couple months after getting her and seeing no change in her demeanor, we hired a trainer. He came to the house, spent about five minutes with her and said, "Where did you get this one?_____ _____,"(Fill in the name of the kennel where we got her from). He asked where she was bred, and I told him that the kennel assured me they only used reputable local breeders. He said I should pursue that one. Remember, I live on Long Island, NY....We finally got the dog's papers. Does Herkimer, Kansas sound local to you? That was my introduction to the world of puppy mills where dogs are bred solely for profit. The parent canines live in small unsanitary cages, with no human interaction. When they can no longer produce a liter, most are just destroyed. Puppies are bred for looks, with no concern about the all-important temperament quality.

Our trainer came several times, and even resorted to a prong collar for the first time in his career. These collars with inward facing prongs are still used today, and can be useful in certain situations. When used properly, they work in training an animal. Failure. The suggestion was made to have the dog used in a junkyard as a guard dog. She was a fear biter with an "I better get you before you get me attitude," which he said would be fine in this type of setting. We couldn't give her up.

We came to love her and she loved us. Even my parents were included into Jetta's pack. My wife got between Jetta and another dog one day and required some stitches, but even this didn't stop us from keeping her. We knew things weren't her fault. The two of us just couldn't bear the thought of adding more misery to her life.

For over eleven years, we never allowed her to come near anyone. Vet visits meant muzzle time, but this professional was still scared of her. We would wait in the car for his signal. Then we would go inside, muzzle her, put her on the table, after which he would make his entrance. She did get to someone at the front door once, and luckily the matter was taken care of without repercussions. When the front door bell rang we would go out through the garage. It's about twenty years since that time and force of habit still keeps us away from the front door in most instances. Old habits stick.

We had Jetta about thirteen years, and finally she developed a spinal/neurological problem, and had to be euthanized. She was buried in the same cemetery as King and Chowder. A sad day for all. While she certainly complicated our life, we loved her dearly, and her love for us in return more than made up for any shortcomings.

Enter the Golden Retriever

A year went by and we were enjoying the freedom of non-dog ownership (like we own them rather than the other way around☺) I think we even took a look at the front door once to see if it still functioned. Yes, life was getting simple. Then we saw a neighbor.

As I mentioned, my parents lived next door to us, and next to them lived a very nice couple whom we knew for many years. Scott was a manager at Home Depot, and one of the people he worked with was breeding golden retrievers. At this point I knew they generally had a good temperament, but to be honest with you I don't believe I could have picked one out of a lineup. That was a little over fourteen years ago. My, how things can change!

Scott and his wife Sue were adopting one of the puppies, and we decided to go over and look at one ourselves. As anyone who has ever gotten a dog can tell you, you do not just go to look at one. If you are sitting there saying, "Why not," it's quite obvious that either you have a will of steel, or you have never engaged in this activity. I'll save you the details and cut to the chase. We were picking up our new family member at the end of the week.

Sue and Scott's dog was named Zoe, and ours we named Shasta. Why Shasta? Here was our reasoning. We liked the name. I guess in our older age we were getting a little boring in the dog naming department.

Zoe was the calm one and ours a bit on the wild side. As I know now, many goldens stay in the wilder puppy stage for a few years. Shasta had her moments, like ripping up the entire new vinyl kitchen flooring one night while we were out, but no real problems. We could even use the front door since she loved everyone. Of course the garage door was still the exit and entrance of choice. Habits die hard.

Shasta was a great dog and friend. She was playful, loved everyone, and rarely caused us any problems. She was a typical golden retriever watchdog. Should a burglar enter the premises, I'm sure she would have licked him, and brought him her stuffed toy before taking him for a guided tour of the house.

Like all dogs, you wind up having to always think about boarding, etc., if you wanted to go somewhere for a few days. We would only board her in one kennel that was about thirty miles from our home. My father had died, and my mother was getting on in years, so other than a trip of a day or two, boarding became necessary. Having Peter Pan syndrome, and never having grown up, Disney was generally where we would go on vacation. We never had children without fur on them, so we couldn't even say it was for the kids. My wife had semi-retired at this time, but since I was still teaching my only options for travel were school holidays when everyone was trying to get away. To get a somewhat reasonable plane flight (remember "no frills", where the fare was low and you were stuffed into the back of the plane and ignored?) you had to make reservations six months in advance. Not a big problem. Accommodations in the Disney area also had to be made even further out. So where was our first call when planning a get-away? You guessed it. The dog kennel, where they were generally booked for up to a year in advance.

At nine and half years of age she suddenly collapsed in the yard. She was running after a squirrel, bumped into a fence very lightly, and the next morning suffered the collapse. We only allow our dogs in the yard when we are actively supervising them, so we couldn't figure out what had happened. An ultrasound revealed liver cancer which had spread.

We always felt that animals do not deserve to suffer. The decision to euthanize should be the answer to one question. Am I keeping the dog alive for my sake or for the dog's sake? Anything other than for the dog sake doesn't seem right. These precious beings have no thoughts of the future. They live for the moment. I asked the veterinarian if Shasta was experiencing any pain at that time. Being told that she wasn't, our thought was, "And she never should." We held her and told her how much we loved her as she gently left this world. Knowing it was the right thing to do does not make it any easier, as anyone suffering the loss of a pet will tell you. Tears fell like rain. Thinking about her still brings forth those drops of moisture. Not a bad thing really. If an animal wasn't as wonderful as it is in life, there would be fewer tears after death. I guess it's sort of a tribute to them, but it doesn't make it any easier. Till the last second her tail was wagging. We humans could learn a lot from that. To live our lives never thinking about yesterday or worrying about tomorrow, and being able to wag our tails even at the moment of death sounds pretty good to me. By this time my wife and I had been Hospice volunteers for quite a few years, and it amazed me how dogs could die with some dignity, but people at times were not allowed to do so. But that's a debate for another time.

Of course this meant another trip to the pet cemetery where our fur child was laid to rest in the double grave with Jetta the German shepherd. If they were in doggie heaven together, there must have been some interesting discussions going on. While one was scarred throughout her life, the other lived each day in joy.

Long Island Golden Retriever Rescue

So, back to the comment I made to my friend at the pool in Florida. The decision not to have another dog was based on two premises. First, we never wanted to go through the pain of losing another canine family member. Second, having only retired a few years before, the prospect of living the life of people who can do what they want, and go where they want, when they want, really appealed to us. Most important was the fact that my mother was about ninety years old at the time. She lived semi-independently in the home next to ours. Separating our properties was a quarter acre of land that we owned, so we built a gravel path through it. As time went on she required more and more assistance, so the path to "grandmutter's" house was used quite a lot. Realizing this need for assistance would only increase, the idea of adding the burden of having a dog was just not for us. All our other furry family members were generally watched over by my mother when we went somewhere. While Mom would still want to take over the role of babysitter, we felt it was just not fair, and perhaps would be dangerous.. What if the dog accidently jumped on her, pulled her down while on a leash, or while serving as a canine speed bump, wound up tripping

Mom when she walked through her own home. These were the reasons why both of us agreed on, "No more dogs."

Do you have any white-out handy? If you do, your assistance here is needed. Please go back to the previous paragraph and white-out words such as we, us, and both. While I knew my wife was not as onboard with the no more dog reasoning, I assumed she accepted it as being a sensible plan at the time. Wrong. Apparently she had been going online for quite some time and looking at a golden retriever rescue group. When first finding out about this, I wondered what the dogs rescued. They are not exactly Saint Bernards with a small barrel around their necks. I was informed that the golden retrievers were themselves "rescued," meaning that they were surrendered by previous owners, or gotten out of shelters and the like. Little did I know how my lack of knowledge in this area was about to change!

Now one thing for sure is that Golden Retrievers are some of the sweetest dogs in town. My reasoning was that if an owner wanted to get rid of one, or if the unfortunate animal wound up in an animal shelter, they probably didn't fit the typical Golden profile. Translation.....problems. Just what we didn't need at this time. As one breeder said to me, "Rescue dogs have issues. While some do have issues, they generally relate to family issues, and in a lot of cases they are medical in nature. The purpose of a rescue group is to take care of these problems so that the dog can find its "forever home."

The website most frequented was one belonging to a group known as "Long Island Golden Retriever Rescue." One day my wife Ronnie got me to look at their website and then came the fateful "click." There on the website menu was a section called, "Available Dogs." We clicked. Well, I had my hand on the mouse. Pretty sure my wife gave my finger a nudge which hit the enter key.

There they were. Several Golden Retrievers varying In ages, each with a few sentence biography under their picture. The "Just Looking," philosophy works about as well on these rescue sites as it does going to a pet store with no intention to buy. In a word....Impossible! Somehow I slowed our "looking" down, and for reasons unknown to me, I randomly clicked on the site a few weeks later. This started the ball rolling.

Charmaine was a couple year old golden who looked so much like Shasta that we both agreed to call and find out more about her. Looking back, I realize that selecting a dog because he or she resembles one you had in the past is sweet, but without much sense behind it. I assume it's our thought that if the dog we had was great and this new one looked the same……well, you can figure out the reasoning here. Without a doubt the fallacy in that theory is quite obvious, but heck, we are only human.

We called the rescue number and spoke to the woman who answered. Turned out to be the president of the group, who to this day basically lives and breathes rescue, and has the phone within an arm's length at all times. We said that we were interested in Charmaine and would like to see her. We were told to first fill out an application and fax it in. Let me tell you the application was extensive to say the least. A million questions, but we assumed it was just routine. A few days went by and we received a call. "Now we get the dog," was certainly what the call was about. Wrong. We were informed that there would now be a volunteer contacting us to do a home visit to see if we qualified. I assumed we were saving a dog that needed a home, and thought that was enough. A few days later a man arrives with several golden retrievers in his car. No doubt one of these was

Charmaine. Nope. They were his dogs that he just brought along for the ride. Did seem like we were getting closer though. At least we saw a few goldens. The home visit went well, and we waited for the phone call. Then we waited some more. We called a couple of times, and were finally told that the dog of our dreams (or so we thought) was being placed with another family. It was hard for us to imagine that we were rejected. Looking back, we now realize that placements are made for the benefit of the dog. In this case the dog's background was more suited to someone else. She might have worked out fine with us, but hey, why not "stack the deck," in terms of the adoption's chance of success. Dogs are not placed on a first come first serve basis, rather on a "compatibility" factor. Sort of like a Match.com for dogs and people.

Golden Eclipse

A week or so went by and hearing nothing we clicked on the Long Island Golden Retriever Rescue (LIGRR) website. There was Eclipse.

A nice looking five year old. We called the organization and were told that they were just checking out a medical issue before adopting out the dog. It still lived with its former owner, who treated it well, so there was no rush. Maybe not for them, but certainly for us.

A few more weeks went by and my wife was close to a breakdown. She sensed we might be approved for this dog, and ran to the phone every time it rang. Around the end of January 2008 we received the call. We were going to meet the dog, the former owner, and the president of LIGRR at a park in Nassau County. Apparently there was a growth or something in Eclipse's mouth, but the group would take care of it either before we took the dog, or after. Not wanting the opportunity to get away from us, we opted for "after."

Arriving early at the park, I noticed a lady walking a golden retriever around the block. After mentioning it to my wife, she asked if I was sure it was the right dog. My response was, "It's either her or two goldens." From the web site picture you could tell she was on the chunky side. Turned out to be a little over a hundred pounds. With the average female golden coming in around seventy, over a hundred was pretty big.

We pulled over and waited by the park. A big sign announced, "No dogs allowed." To this day we still refer to it as "No Dogs Allowed Park." The rescue president pulled up and we waited for the twosome to make their way around the block. Eclipse seemed nice. We were all talking in the street and she just laid down in the road as if it was no big deal. Just struck us as unusual. New people, new environment, and you just lay down in the middle of the street, with cars zipping by less than a foot away, unconcerned? Not exactly typical canine behavior to say the least. We were to learn that for her nothing was a big deal. There was a good size lump on the inside of her mouth about the size of a large grape, but the rescue group was taking care of it, so no big deal. Melanie (the president) asked what we thought of the dog. My wife said, "She's wonderful." Done deal. She jumped into the back seat (where we had a doggie hammock set up) of our Prius. For the forty mile or so trip home she just laid peacefully in the back looking at us with an expression that sort of said, "You guys look OK, and I guess my new life is going to start"

Apparently there was a complete lunar eclipse a day or so after Eclipse was born. While not a bad name for a dog, I'm glad the title of this book isn't Golden Lunar. My wife always wanted to shorten her name to "Clipse," but somehow I had the feeling that she would resent being called Onnie, while Oward wasn't my name either☺

One side note that you might find interesting. A few years before, my wife was taking a ferry home from Connecticut to Long Island. She met a woman on the boat who had a golden retriever with her. Apparently the woman was coming to the island to stay with her daughter. My wife told her that she had never seen a dog act so calm. Eclipse's age, previous owner's reason for giving her up etc., makes her feel fairly confident that she had met Eclipse before. You never know.

Eclipse at Home

It was a Sunday afternoon when we arrived home. Here was an older dog who had just left its home, ridden in a car with strangers, and was about to go into a totally new situation. We worried about how she would react to her new surroundings. Basically she didn't. She comes inside, looks around and lies down. By our front door we have about a five by eight section of tiles. We noticed that at one point she walked over and laid down on them, positioning herself so that her back was along the bottom edge of the front door. Reminded me of one of those stuffed three foot things you buy to lay against the inside edge of a door in winter to protect against drafts. My wife felt she knew what was going on. Eclipse missed her old master, and was waiting for her by the door. So sad. Of course after four years of Eclipse continuing this behavior, we came up with a different conclusion. She liked the draft and the cool tiles. Sometimes we tend to dig too deeply into the hidden meanings of things. A human characteristic, but one we maybe shouldn't automatically extend to a dog's actions.

One thing I felt would really be disorienting for the new dog would be following a Sunday tradition. My mother loved to cooked....let's make that she lived to cook. She always said that growing up during the depression years when food was scarce made her appreciate food, not just as something to be taken for granted, but rather to be appreciated. Mom always described it as, "God's food." Now I don't want you to get the idea that since the three of us normally had dinner together that she was preparing food for three. After sitting down, out would come enough quantity and variety of food to feed ten people who haven't eaten in a week. Quality was understood. We would always leave her home on Sunday evenings with enough leftover food to feed us for most of the upcoming week. Trust me when I say that is not an exaggeration. Mom was always preparing food for all of her friends and for anyone that needed a helping hand. This from a woman over ninety years old!

After living in a nice home for years, we took Eclipse in a strange vehicle, took her for a long ride, and then brought her into our place. Talk about changes for the poor animal. You would think she would be so torn up inside, with all the changes, not knowing what was going on. Sorry. Here I go again giving human attributes to a dog. I'm in no way saying that human attributes are better than canine ones, just different. After being in this new environment for an hour or so, the thought of again giving her a change by taking her to Mom's for dinner didn't seem right. Of course saying no to Mom and her Sunday dinner didn't seem right either, since she just about lived for and prepared for this event all week. So we put on Eclipse's leash and over we went.

Can you just imagine what this poor animal did when we got there? She lies down and relaxes. When we went into the dining room to eat she came in with us but never begged for food. Everything went well, and we returned home a few hours later with our new friend and fifty pounds of leftovers. Her previous owner gave us the dog's bed, and I placed it next to my side of our bed. She laid down and went to sleep. My wife and I couldn't believe how she seemed to be adapting to a totally new situation. As we were to learn, adapting is what Eclipse was an expert at. Just about nothing bothered her.

One incident struck us as rather different. The first evening Eclipse was with us, my wife went in the den to watch television. The dog jumps up on the couch next to my wife, and lies down. A short time later she gets down, and never again went on any piece of furniture! Never could figure out the meaning behind that behavior.

You have never seen a dog age as quickly as Eclipse. When we picked her up, her paperwork listed her as a five year old. Upon further checking, the fact that her first couple years were spent as a breeding dog was omitted. This meant that she was really over seven years of age. If a person were to find out that they were really about fifty percent older that they thought they were, it would probably upset them. Upset wouldn't even begin to describe the emotions they would feel! Of course to a dog, it's no big thing. Another canine advantage. We may be the superior species, but at times, I think that's because humans are the ones that declared us to be. Other species no doubt see things differently.

So here we are. The third family that this poor animal has known. We were dedicated to making this her "forever home," and a home filled with love and care. Little did we know that she apparently had the same thoughts in mind in terms of filling our lives with love and care.

Mouth Bump

So here we are at about day three. We're simply amazed at Eclipse. She is all we could ever dream of in terms of the perfect dog. Housetrained, gentle, calm, and any other word you can come up with that you feel would describe an amazing canine that you would love to call your own. Even her eating habits surprised us. Why? She ate like a Golden Retriever. The literal translation of eating like a Golden is that a dog inhales their food in about ten seconds and burps afterwards. Our last golden would sometimes go for a day or so without eating. Not due to illness. Food consumption to her was just not important. Before you begin wondering if it was the menu that was causing the problem, be aware that we tried homemade food, pork fried rice from the neighborhood Chinese restaurant, and other cuisines that a gourmet would be proud of! Shasta may eat one of these items for a day or so, but without enthusiasm, but that would be about it. She was simply more interested in exploring and playing than in eating. Here we were, with Eclipse, going from a non-eater to a dog that lived to eat. Quite refreshing.

Of course there was one "minor" thing to take care of. That growth in her mouth had to be looked at. The rescue group sent us to one of their vets. Even sitting in the waiting room, we were to see interesting behavior. Out of the back room comes a five or ten pound little dog, who decides to basically climb all over Eclipse's face. Her reaction? None. She just stands there. Now don't get me wrong. It's not that she was being submissive, more like understanding. I know it's a stretch assigning a quality such as that to a dog, but if you had been there you would have agreed. It's like she said to herself, "He doesn't mean it. He just came from the examining room and is a bit excited." Before you think I'm going off the deep end describing this, let me again say that you had to be there to believe it! We were to learn that this was only a preview of her amazing nature.

The veterinarian came out of the back room to take a quick look at the growth and basically sign off on it. One look and he said it was not quite what he was expecting, and would have to anesthetize her and take some samples. The procedure was to take a couple of hours. We went to a local burger place to wait it out. While sitting there we came to a definite conclusion. Eclipse was with us for the long haul. We were going to be her forever home regardless of the biopsy outcome.

The results came back. It was a benign, but highly aggressive cancer that was growing into the bone. Serious surgery was the only way to get rid of it. A week later we were meeting in a veterinary specialty practice with two oncologists, a surgeon, and the president of the rescue group. The decision was made that the poor dog needed something called a hemi-mandiblectomy, which requires the removal of a number of teeth and a good size section of jawbone. As part of her initial testing upon entering rescue she was routinely checked for thyroid conditions. No problem was found. Melanie, the president, told the doctors she wanted a retest. Why? Here were a whole bunch of us in a tiny exam room and Eclipse is simply laying out on the floor resting as if nothing is going on. Obviously an underactive thyroid. No, obviously a normal Eclipse, who would face a situation like this with a more or less, "I'll just relax here and I'm sure they will tell me what's coming next attitude." You can guess the results of the test. Negative thyroid problem. The mouth surgery was scheduled about two weeks down the road.

A Life Changing Experience

I had been a Hospice patient volunteer for quite a long time. About a week after Eclipse arrived at our home, I was speaking with a patient's family, and setting up a date for a home visit. At some point in the conversation, the fact that we had adopted a dog came up. The gentleman loved dogs, and they would really like me to bring her along on my upcoming visit. This presented a bit of a quandary to me. One of the main goals of the hospice programs is to give the patients anything they request that will bring some joy and comfort into their lives. On the other hand, to bring an animal that I only met a week or so before into an unknown environment, filled with medical devices and the like, was a bit of a risk. I knew she was a good girl, well behaved and everything, but with the medical aspect, all bets were off. I made the decision to give it a try, since I could remove her from the situation should anything undesirable occur. This decision to take her on the visit literally changed Eclipse's and my life for the next four and a half years!

The day of the visit we head out. Still not knowing what exactly to expect, I was, of course, a little on edge. I didn't exactly think Eclipse would attack anyone, or cause a scene. Rather, I was worried that the combination of a new environment, new individuals, and a home set up to supply medical care to a terminally ill person might be rather traumatic for her. As I was to find out, over the coming months and years, a thermonuclear device exploding near her would be about the only thing that could upset her. Mainly because of the fact that her next meal would, in all probability, be postponed!

Getting out of the car, I put her on a short lease, and hoped all would go well. I know the visit meant a lot to the patient, and would have hated to have to cut the visit short should a problem develop. In we go. The patient is in his chair. His wife and an aide are also in the room. At this point he could not move too much without assistance, and any movements were not well coordinated. This could make petting the dog a bit awkward for both him and the dog. How does Eclipse handle a strange medical environment, with three new people? I remembered reading that dogs can tell if a person is ill, so it would seem to follow that a terminally ill person must elicit an even more intense reaction. In a way I was right. What does she do? She simply walked slowly through the room, over to the patient, and lies down on the floor next to him, right next to his arm which was dangling over the arm of the chair. You might be able to train a dog to do this, but in this case, it simply seemed like she intuitively knew the right thing to do.

Naturally, the rest of the visit went well and then another rather amazing thing happened. As we got ready to leave I jokingly said, "It's time to go, say good-bye to everyone." And she did! Eclipse went to each person in the room who reached down and petted her. She was not a jumper or a licker, but merely stood there as if saying good-bye. After going to the final person, she walks over to me with an expression on her face that said, "OK, I'm ready to leave." I should stress at this point that after being used for breeding at a young age, she had lived with a woman in a normal home setting. No special training of any kind took place. We all just stood there looking at her. Really nothing could be said. I'm sure a lot of different thoughts were going through our minds, but words simply could not do justice to what just transpired. Out to the car we went. I couldn't wait to get home to tell my wife about the visit. It was fairly obvious though that this was one of those, "You had to see it to believe it encounters." Oh yeah, one more thing happened at the end of the visit that was to repeat itself many times during the next four and half years. The patient's family said they would really appreciate another visit from Eclipse. Please note that they did not say, "We would appreciate another visit from you and please bring the dog." From this day on I was to hear similar expressions from many people. Sure put me in my place…..and I wouldn't have had it any other way. Being second fiddle to this amazing canine was not a put down. She could play first fiddle. I would always be honored to just be a part of her band.

Eclipse had her major surgery a couple of weeks after this visit. The gentleman we had visited had a great deal of problems communicating orally. I was watching the dog carefully since we just arrived home from the hospital a day or so before, when the phone rang. It was the wife of the Hospice patient. Apparently her husband asked her to, "Find out about Eclipse." This touched me deeply, and further demonstrated the remarkable impact she could make in people's lives

Not a Human Hospital.....Thankfully

We, of course, were worried about the procedure, which was not a simple one by any means. For the two weeks leading up to the surgery we were just hoping that all would go well. During this time we took her to a local Petco where dogs are allowed in the store. After telling the manager of the upcoming operation, Eclipse left the store with a huge bag of complimentary treats, and the instructions, "Give the poor baby whatever she wants." To Eclipse, who lived to eat, there could not have been a better set of instructions.

The big day had arrived and we drove the forty miles or so to the veterinary hospital. It was early morning, and she was taken into the back room to be prepped. We sat in the waiting room with no intention of leaving. Luckily the hospital was open twenty four hours, because if that's how long we had to wait to find out how she was doing we would have!

After what seemed like an eternity, the surgeon came out and said that everything had gone well, and that Eclipse was in the recovery room. More time passed and we were told that she was in ICU, and would be there till morning. Our first thought was, "ICU?" Sure enough. They took us into a room with several large cages around the outside, and a manned nursing station in the middle filled with monitors. We were able to go home feeling fairly confident that she was in good hands. Needless to say, we would be returning early the next morning.

Bright and early we were back at the hospital. Now comes something that is going to seem like total fiction. It's not. A setup like I am about to describe really does exist. Unfortunately not for humans!

If you were ever admitted to a hospital, I'm sure you were concerned about more than one or two issues besides your physical care. Being in a strange and somewhat impersonal place, your world changes. Here you are in a difficult environment, maybe even recovering from a surgical procedure, and of course, you are separated for most of the time from family members who love you and wished they could stay by your side constantly to administer the loving care that only they can provide. In a hospital you have no doubt heard those medical infusion machines that drip medicine into a person's arm. If a problem with the drip occurs they go beep, and beep and beep, and then they beep! I'm sure you have probably heard this annoying sound in your lifetime.

Theory has it, that the beep will alert a nurse, who will immediately rush to your side, make adjustments, and above all provide needed reassurances. Yes, that's the theory. Unfortunately, as those of you have been hospitalized are more than aware, this is not often the case. Those beeps can go on forever until someone finally comes in. There you are in bed, not exactly feeling chipper, wondering why this thing is beeping, and most of all, wondering why no one on the medical staff is interested in either finding out the reason, or at least stopping the annoying sound. The beeps are meant to be annoying so they will gain the attention of medical personnel. Unfortunately, many times the only people whose attention is gotten are you, your roommate, and anyone in adjacent rooms. Seems like the only people who are able to ignore it are those who shouldn't. This is not to say that they don't care. They are generally understaffed and simply cannot be everywhere at once. Part of my volunteer work at Hospice was doing something called a "death vigil." Basically I would stay with a patient while family members got a break, or sometimes overnight, so the patient would not die alone. From this experience I can tell you that the ignored beeping machines are, unfortunately, all too common.

Luckily for Eclipse, she was not human! We were ushered into a room that contained two reclining lounges (Barkolounges?), a desk, internet access, a television, a table, a thickly padded dog bed (which to be honest took up a good portion of the room, and a large supply of warm blankets. Two infusion machines were in the room as well.

Our girl was brought in wearing one of those Elizabethan collars like you see on dogs that just "got fixed," and her IV's were hooked up to the machines. (Always struck me as strange that being spayed or neutered is referred to as being fixed, when there is nothing broken in the first place, but there sure is after the surgery!). There were a few rooms in a circular pattern around a nursing station located in the center. Being the only patient in this area she actually had a private nurse. During the day the surgeon and others were in and out to check on her condition. All was going quite well. Eclipse was obviously a little "drugged," and just rested comfortably on her plush bed. My wife and I sat on our lounges. For most of the day I reached out my hand and touched my little girl. I'm pretty sure the contact comforted her. One thing was certain. It comforted me.

Unlike a human hospital, we were spending the night in her private room. She was generally sleeping at the end of her bed right next to my chair. Of course this meant that I was obligated to maintain contact with her throughout the night. Some might say that obligated is a bit of a strong word to use in this situation. To true dog lovers it fits just perfectly! A couple of times during the night one of the IV's would fall out, or medication would run out, causing the machines to make that annoying sound. Of course since this was a dog hospital and not a human one, a couple of beeps were all a person had to put up with, since the nurse outside the room came running in to straighten out the situation. At one point Eclipse made a little sound that seemed to be a cry. In comes the nurse who checks her out and assures us that it was a happy, drug induced cry, not one associated with pain. If we had taken her home that evening we would have been rushing back to the vet rather that reclining in our chairs feeling good that Eclipse was feeling good.

In the middle of the night I took the patient outside to relieve herself. I kind of lost my sense of direction since the hospital had many twists and turns. Believe it or not, Eclipse takes over, and walks purposefully down the hallways to her room. Sort of a canine GPS.

One thing I could have used was a massage, after spending the night bent over the end of the chair to maintain contact. A massage was given by a member of the hospital staff. Really! In the morning came the massage. It was not for me, but for Eclipse. Did make me feel good though, seeing her receive it.

Passing the Food Test

The next morning my wife had to leave for an appointment, and I was to stay for the day, waiting for her to return late in the afternoon, when hopefully the three of us would be returning home. One of the nurses (I realize that the expression vet-tech would probably be technically correct, but at this facility, nurse is much closer to reality) told me that she couldn't be discharged until they could be sure she was able to eat. Now with food consumption her primary reason for existing, I doubted if there would be a problem. They took some dog food and made doggie meatballs out of it. Did she eat? Don't be silly. Here she was with the giant cone on her head swallowing meatballs like they were from a fancy Italian restaurant. I thought it would be interesting to simply roll one from the outside of the cone to the inside where she could just open her mouth and let it slide in it, but never really implemented this technique.

Late in the day we loaded the patient into the car, and home we went. Upon arriving she simply walked inside like nothing had happened and settled right back into her normal routine. Dogs just move on with life. They do not think of yesterday or tomorrow, but instead concentrate on the moment. Our species might view this as narrow minded, but in many ways it seems to be an amazing way to face life.

For the next month or so our kitchen turned into a doggie meatball factory. Eclipse acted like her usual self at all times, even climbing up the stairs with her huge, satellite dish looking collar on. I'm still not totally sure how she accomplished this feat. Subsequent visits to the veterinary hospital showed that healing was taken place, and biopsies demonstrated that the cancer had not spread. All great news. A month after her surgery I even invested a couple thousand dollars and had a renowned "doggie dentist" clean her teeth, remove a few small growths, and generally evaluate her mouth. This took another whole day where I stayed in the waiting room. She stays, I stay! It's as simple as that. Upon her release later in the day I was presented with a chart describing the condition of every tooth in her mouth.....those that were left anyway. I was also presented with a dog whose teeth had gone from dismal looking, to being able to model for a toothpaste company.

Little Drifter

The dentist noted that with a sizable piece of jawbone missing Eclipse could not function successfully in the eating category. This made me laugh, since I knew this activity was her forte. He suggested bone grafts, and implants. Pricy, but supposedly necessary. Or so I was told. She had what is known as mandible drift, meaning that the bottom jaw just "drifted" to the side since there was a lack of jawbone to support it. Decisions had to be made.

I spoke to quite a number of people, and researched the procedure without reaching any definite conclusion. My mind was made up by the surgeon who performed the hemi-madiblectomy and my local veterinarian who is extremely competent and caring. I assured the surgeon that I respected the dentist's opinion, and that my object was not to cause trouble between them, but merely to get a second opinion, or in this case a seventh. I can still remember her words, which could easily be transferred to human medicine and the treatment options that we are sometimes given. She said," In medicine there are things that you can do, but that doesn't mean you should." Having been a Hospice volunteer for over fifteen years, and having interacted with many individuals who were facing decisions about treatment options, the relevance of her statement was obvious.

In Hospice, we, on occasion, have a patient who comes into our program literally hours before dying. The whole concept of the program is to provide palliative care to end of life patients, and to offer family support. By combinations of nurses, volunteers, social workers, pastoral care specialists, and pain management experts, we are able to make an individual's last weeks or months, ones which include comfort, both physical and mental, and dignity. Something that is many times lost in a medical setting. Why do some of our patients only benefit from our services for a few hours? Because some doctors want to try "one more thing." Many view the death of their patient as a failure on their part, rather than accepting it as a natural consequence of being human. They are trained to save lives, and receive little if any training on "letting go, "and Hospice care. As the saying goes, "No one ever made it out of this life alive.

If you will allow me to step off my soapbox, I'll return to the original theme of this chapter. In the preface you were told that I was not a professional writer. If I was I would have stayed on topic, and not included the last paragraph. Since you were properly warned, I cannot be held accountable. Eat your heart out Stephen King. Actually I wouldn't doubt it if someone did eat their heart out in one of his books.

I know, I know. What did the local veterinarian say? Somehow I still remember her words to this day. "You may be opening up a can of worms that you won't be able to close." I could probably go off into another topic where these words would also apply, but I won't." You're welcome.

The decision was made to not do, "what could be done," and to "leave the worms in the can." A wise decision. Probably the only negative was that Eclipse was not supposed to eat anything hard like a big biscuit, rawhide, or the like. Obviously chewing on doggie toys was out. Since she had no interest in toys of any kind, that wasn't going to be a problem. I'm sure her reasoning was simply. "You can't eat a toy, therefore it has no purpose." Once in a while someone would give her a large biscuit before I could stop them. Being such a thoughtful animal, and not wanting to hurt their feelings, she would eat it. Very considerate of her, and no damage was ever done.

I used to buy small wheat free puppy biscuits that she loves. She would have to grab for them a bit with the lopsided jaw, but never caused any damage. Many people said her jaw gave her added personality, and my favorite observation made by quite a number of individuals was that she had an "Elvis Sneer." Our vet used to refer to her as my "little drifter." All in all, leaving the jaw drifting, rather than doing the risky jaw reconstruction seemed to be the correct decision.

Therapy Dog?

After the visit to the Hospice patient I did some research. I had remembered reading about dogs that were specifically trained to interact with patients, and bring some joy into their lives. Apparently they were called therapy dogs. Looking into it further I found out that any dog could become certified to perform this service. Requirements to obtain the certification however, were quite stringent. A candidate had to know all the obedience commands, such as sit, down, stay, come, etc. They also had to interact well with other dogs, and above all show the ability to "maintain their cool," when faced with walkers, patients with canes, medical machinery, and all the noise that they entail. Patients who may not have the ability to interact normally with the animal are another problem for some candidates. Not meaning to do so, a patient might have physical problems which could result in their petting the dog too hard, pulling an ear, etc. Somehow the dog must realize that they must not react adversely to situations such as these. The amount of canines that can fulfill all of the requirements is relatively small, as you can readily imagine. But as they say, "Nothing ventured, nothing gained." An organization known as Therapy Dogs International seemed to be one of the premier organizations that certifies the animals. Their website listed in detail the requirements and testing dates. I chose a testing date several months out and began the training process. You can have someone train the dog for you, but somehow I had a deep down feeling that Eclipse and I would just work well together as a team, and could teach each other to achieve all of the requirements.

Bad Temperament

A couple of weeks after starting training, Eclipse went in for her surgery. After coming home I did a little bit of training with her, but not much since major surgery, and rigorous training, didn't seem to be a good combination. Rest made sense to me. Then my wife came home with some interesting news from a friend of hers. The event that followed gave us many laughs during the next four years. People who I shared the story with simply shook their heads, while generally making a comment which boiled down to, "Are you kidding…. Eclipse?"

My wife's friend had heard about a local veterinarian who had his own therapy dog program, and was holding tryouts in two days. Dogs that passed his screening process would be enrolled in his training program and then be sent out to do therapy…..sort of. Figuring that it certainly couldn't hurt to have Eclipse enrolled in a training program, I took her to the evaluation meeting. There were about eight of us there as I remember. We met my wife's friend in the parking lot beforehand. Here was her young dog bouncing around, and mine simply laying there relaxing. She was worrying about her dog not being accepted into training, and wished that she would act more like my partner, who would obviously be accepted into the program. Need I say who was accepted and who was rejected for having a "bad temperament?"

First came a general meeting with the owners and the vet without the dogs, where the program was explained to us. A couple of things bothered me. Apparently anyone going through his training course was obligated to work a specified amount of times. This made sense since you were receiving free training. What sort of rubbed me the wrong way was that he was charging groups who received the therapy and then donating it to a local charity that he worked with. Just seemed a little tacky to me, but not ridiculous. I was aware that Therapy Dogs International was a worldwide, well respected organization which had existed for many years. They were so confident that a dog that could pass their strict exam would perform its duties at a high level, and that there would never be any behavior issues, each dog was actually insured up to one million dollars should an incident arise. Just that alone tells you how seriously they take certification. I did ask the veterinarian what group certifies his dogs and his response was, "I do." It did not seem quite the same.

After the owners met we were to meet with the veterinarian one on one with our dogs in an exam room for more intensive evaluation. Here is Eclipse, a couple of weeks or so after major surgery being pushed around on the floor by a stranger in an exam room. She was so cooperative that he even called his vet tech in to show her how he was literally using the dog as a pillow. This is when Eclipse showed her bad temperament. He had me sit in a chair with her beside me. Walking over he takes the leash from me and tells me to remain seated while he takes the dog away into the back room. Now here is my poor girl who just had a not fun experience in a veterinary hospital a couple of weeks before being led to another room by a stranger. Eclipse simply pushed herself into my side and as we came to call it, "Put on the breaks." No aggression, growling, etc. I'm sure he could have dragged her or kicked her into the next room and she wouldn't have done anything negative. It was at this point that he informed me that Eclipse had just failed his evaluation and she would not be eligible for his program along with the included training due to the fact that she had a bad temperament, as demonstrated by her refusal to go with him. I didn't see the relevance of this to being a therapy dog, but what did I know. Out to the parking area we go where most of the other dogs, including my wife's friend's young active dog were celebrating their acceptance into the program. I loaded my bad temperament dog into the car and off we went. I called the office the next day and asked if I could pay to take the course and they agreed that it would be possible. Training to help us prepare for the TDI test in a few months would probably be quite beneficial.

Over the next few months I asked some testers from Therapy Dogs International about this evaluation, and generally their response was that you don't want a dog who will go into shall we say a nursing home situation and just go away with anyone who tries to take her. The handler should always be the one to take the dog to a person who wishes to see her, and never should the dog "just go" with someone." Makes sense, no?

A couple of days after receiving the disqualification I get a call that was to lead to something I never would have expected, although with Eclipse I should have. My apologies, girl.

TDI Test

So here I am at home with my bad temperament dog who failed to even pass her evaluation to be considered for training. While a little disheartened, I felt that I should still try to get us ready for our Therapy Dog International Test which was to be held in a few months. Even if we didn't make it, certainly the training time spent together would be well worth it. Good plan, right? Then the phone rings.

Who is calling? It's the tester from TDI telling me that an opening just occurred in her testing schedule, and she could move Eclipse's evaluation up. The new test would take place in a week or so. My first thought was, "No way!" Reconsidering, I decided to go with it. My decision was based on two factors. One was that while we obviously wouldn't pass, I could get a good idea of our main areas of weakness, and then spend the next couple of months working on them. The other was an assurance that we could retake the exam at the normal time originally scheduled several months hence.

One correction should be made at this point. I do not want you to get the idea that the training is just for the dog. TDI does not certify dogs. It certifies therapy teams made up of a handler and a dog. Both must perform at high standards. Even if a dog qualifies, he or she cannot do therapy work with anyone other than the person who passed the test with the animal. So, by taking this earlier exam we would find out team weaknesses that needed attention, not canine weakness. A big difference!

Here it was. The morning of our team's evaluation. An overcast day loomed ahead. We set out to the testing area which was about forty miles away. I realized that it was to be held outdoors, but had no idea it was held in conjunction with some large scale dog event. We are directed to park in a field and around us are many cars, many people, and many, many dogs. One thing I noticed about Eclipse was that she liked to go and see other dogs. She would just want to say hello to them. To my dismay, one part of the exam involves us walking toward another team. When we get next to each other the human components shake hands and start a discussion. All the while, our canine buddies are supposed to just stand or sit there ignoring each other. I knew this was going to be difficult. Getting from the car to the test area about a hundred feet away involved passing several dogs, all of whom wanted to meet Eclipse and vice versa.

It should be stressed that during the exam you are not permitted to pull on a dog's leash, yell at them or anything of the sort. (Not that I would ever yell at my little girl☺) The idea is that they, as equal team members, can take care of themselves.

While waiting for the testing sessions to begin, I did two things. One will seem normal and one certainly won't. Normal first. Standing by a group of people I get involved in the conversation. Mentioning that I was there for the therapy dog testing one of the people asked who the evaluator was. A few frowns followed when I read her name from my signup sheet. They wished me luck, and said not to be disappointed since she was one of the toughest evaluators in the program. Good news for the program and probably bad news for us. Oh yeah, the not so normal thing. I took a bag of liver treats, crumbled them up, and basically washed my hands with them! The rules stated that food rewards may not be used during testing, but no one ever said anything about food smells. My reasoning was that while Eclipse always paid attention to me, this wonderful aroma I would give off couldn't hurt!

I noticed several people lining up to sign in for the test. A lady with a well behaved dog was in front of me talking to the evaluator. To this day I remember the conversation. She said that her dog already did nursing home visits, and was well behaved. She just wanted to get official certification. The evaluator's response was something to the effect that she didn't really care what the dog had done before. Not exactly comforting for me to hear.

Realizing that we were almost last on the testing schedule would give us hopefully an hour to just chill out and relax before our big moment came. My thought was still that this evaluation would show me some of our areas of weakness that we could focus on in preparation for our "real" test in a few months.

First up were a teenage girl and her big white dog. Apparently the first item on the agenda was for this team to meet another team, where the dogs would ignore each other. Not a typical canine behavior. Now for the interesting turn of events. This testing item obviously needed another team, and you can, without a doubt, guess who the evaluator told to get out there and meet the other team. Eclipse and myself. Oh, great! I guess in a way it was good to get this over with. From about thirty feet away we start walking towards each other. When we are a foot or so apart we stop and shake hands and talk for a few minutes (the human component☺) Eclipse sat down next to me, as did the other dog by the young girl. Unbelievably they both just remained there and actually turned their heads to the side so as not to even be looking at each other. Call it luck, fate, or as I chose to look at it, Eclipse just somehow knowing what was required of her, our two teams could have been on a video used to demonstrate the "meet and greet."

When our time for testing came up, it had just started to drizzle, with a forecast of heavy rain at any moment. By now you have probably surmised how things went from this point on. Sit, stay, down, people patting her hard and not in a usual manner (to simulate possible nursing home resident behavior) others running around her, using walkers and canes right in front of her face, etc., was handled in a perfect manner. Well, I must admit there was one screw-up. At one point a dog biscuit is put on the ground. We were to walk by it, wherein I would say, "Leave it," and on we would go. Twice I made the mistake of stopping after giving the command rather than just moving on. If only I had Eclipse's innate ability to get things right! By now it was raining quite heavy, and we had only one more section of the test to complete. To be sure the dog can stand being separated from the human, I was to give the leash to someone, and proceed to walk out of sight, and remain there for several minutes until called back. During this time the dog should not pull on the leash, bark, or act up in any way. Here's Eclipse under a canopy that was set up out of the rain, while I'm standing in a field some distance away, drowning. When the time was up and I returned, the evaluator said she did fine. Let's see.. I'm in the field drowning and she's under the canopy. She's certainly smart enough to know who had it better.

At the bottom of the evaluation form there is an area where the test administrator writes comments on areas of strengths and weaknesses, along with a final determination of competence. As previously mentioned, dogs serving as part of TDI certified teams are insured up to one million dollars against anything that might happen when serving in nursing homes, etc. Naturally TDI does not want an unstable team out there in the world. I was handed my final evaluation where all areas were checked off as satisfactory. There in the comments section was one word, written large. It was the same word that my wife said to the president of LIGRR when asked what she thought of the dog we had just met. "WONDERFUL!"

I'll never forget the pride I felt at that moment. By this point we looked like drown rats from all the rain. Bodies dampened, but spirits soaring, we walked proudly back to the car to return home, now a certified therapy dog team. Upon arriving home, my wife took one look at Eclipse in her soggy condition and said, "She looks like she is saying, "I passed my test and I'm so proud," May sound anthropomorphic, but she was right. Without a doubt that was the look on her face! A rescue dog in her third home for only a few weeks, still recovering from major cancer surgery, not to mention being labeled as having a bad temperament, had just completed a very difficult evaluation by a known tough evaluator with flying colors. What can I say? WONDERFUL!!

Fund Raising

So here is my new best friend, a registered therapy dog, and now pretty well-healed from her major surgery. Since the rescue group spent many thousands on her care, we felt we had an obligation to repay the favor by doing a little volunteer work for them. Little did I know where this would eventually lead.

There is a huge furniture store in the area where they were allowing the group to bring a few dogs to do some fund raising. The place is so big that they actually have a food area where they give out coffee, hot dogs, ice cream, etc. Even some face painting going on for the kids. This is where we were stationed. When we arrived there were about three other dogs there. Eclipse walks over to them, goes up to meet each one, and then just lies down next to me. I was to learn that this behavior would be repeated many times. Several hours past and I never once had to stop Eclipse from doing anything wrong. Improper behavior was just not in her list of available behaviors. Never did I have to worry about her wandering away, jumping on someone, or any of the other behaviors that are common to even the best of dogs. We left feeling that some of our debt to the organization was repaid. Little did I know this was just the first installment? Many more "payments, "were to come, and would continue to this day.

Starbucks

Writing this section anywhere would be difficult for me. Eclipse had just left this world a week before I wrote it. There is one place where writing it would be unbearable. Yes, that's where I'm writing it! Just couldn't do it anywhere else. Hopefully I can finish before the tears short circuit my laptop.

My wife plays a lot of tennis with her friends and I like to drop her off, spend an hour and a half reading a book in Starbucks, and then go pick her up. A couple of weeks after we got Eclipse....or vice versa....I took her along since she was such a great rider. The weather was cool so there was no problem leaving her alone in the car. I parked where I could keep a constant eye on her. No problems. Not that I expected any.

A few weeks after this I began working with my girl to become a therapy dog team. I even picked up a vest that said, "Therapy Dog in Training." I figured she would look official and wanted to give something a try.

I with my Hospice badge, and her with her vest, walked into Starbucks. What the heck. Nothing ventured, nothing gained. It was pretty crowded, but I found an empty seat and sat down.

She sat next to me. My concern was going up to get my coffee when it was ready. Up I go, and Eclipse? She just lies down by the chair and keeps her eyes on me. Returning to my seat I notice people looking at her, probably thinking me a highly skilled dog trainer. You cannot train a dog to behave like her. Bothering other people, walking around Starbucks and such, would be a sign of disrespect. Simply not in her repertoire. The place could be super busy and kids could be running all over, but Eclipse simply had the," It has nothing to do with me, "mindset.

Once in a great while I would have to go to Starbucks without her. I'd walk in and all the employees would ask, "Where is Eclipse?" If she was the only one to enter it is highly doubtful that anyone would ask….or care, "Where is Howard?" I was always aware of my place in the pack.

We had by this time just about eliminated verbal communication between us. She never barked, and I rarely had to give instructions to her. It's like we both instinctively knew what to do when together. When leaving Starbucks I would make little clicking sounds. I can never remember how this "click," thing started. She would get up, stretch and out we would go.

Where I went, she went. If places didn't want her to enter, then that meant they didn't want me there either! Just the way it was. Probably the only time I was questioned was heading into a Sam's Club one afternoon. The person who checks your pass at the door gave the dog a look and said, "Seeing Eye Dog?"

Now I am not the kind of person who would ever tell a lie about something like that, so of course my response was, "Yes." Once we got inside my wife gives me this look and says, "Seeing Eye Dog?" My comeback was, "Yes, seeing eye dog, smelling nose dog, hearing ear dog, etc. "I guess I misunderstood the person at the door." All Right, not really.

Hospice Therapy Dog

So here we were. A registered Therapy Dog Team. Supposedly we were equal team members, but as I was to find out, there was a leader and an assistant in this partnership. Guess I should have realized this by noting that we were a therapy DOG Team, not a therapy HUMAN team.

In my many years as a Hospice patient volunteer, the organization did not have a certified team. We were the first, and so far the last the organization utilized. We would go to see patients in their homes. Not to brag, but we made an awesome difference in many lives. Well, ok, Eclipse did.

Here were families going through one of the roughest periods of time in their lives. The patent is in the last days or weeks of their life. The family is there trying to offer all the support possible, while trying to hold things together in their own lives. These areas are where Hospice helps out. We supply all medical equipment for the home, regular nurse, social worker, and spiritual visits as needed, and most importantly as requested. Twenty four hour on call nurses are also available. We do not enter a home with an agenda other than to do all we can to assist everyone involved in the end of life process. Some families want tremendous support, while others do not. We can make suggestions, but they make all final decisions. Quite a number of families and/or patients do not want the word dying mentioned. Fine. After all, the family has been a unit with their own values that they have come to share over the years. We are the new kids on the block, and must respect their wishes at all times.

Another component of the program is the volunteers. We are trained to offer whatever support we can. I have found over the years that often times while not professionals, we can offer support not readily found in the medical community. Most of the time, members of the Hospice team are asking questions, doing medical testing, etc. But, on the other hand, as volunteers, we are just there with no specific agenda. We just walk in, sit down, and take it from there. So often I have found that patients and family members tell us things that they never mention to the regular hospice staff. This is probably due to the fact we are "unofficial," with a role simply to being there to help. I have cut bushes, discussed life and death, gone shopping, and stayed with a patient so a caregiver could get some free time for themselves. A tremendously important thing for them to have!

Now if I am unofficial, think of Eclipse. She really walks in with zero preconceptions, and certainly with only one thing on her agenda. Just to be there and share unconditional love. I have seen patients who have not smiled in quite some time get the biggest expression of joy on their face when she walks in. Sometimes they talk to her, or just hold her. Words are not needed by canines. They are used by us to communicate our thoughts and feelings. Dogs can do this instantly, so why bother with cumbersome words? I used to get the biggest laugh out of what would generally happen at the end of our visits. The family and patient would ask when Eclipse could come back. Carefully note the question did not include my name. Such a tribute to the power of love that she was able to transmit to people without words. Perhaps a lesson for humans here?

While Eclipse made an awesome difference in many lives, the next few chapters will highlight just a few examples of this.

Now, Official Visits

One family I was assigned to was the same family I had visited with Eclipse after having her for only a week. The elderly husband was dying, and his wife and a live in aide, as well as other family members, were taking great care of him

We made quite a few visits to this family. Eclipse demonstrated behavior that no one could have taught her. It's like she just instinctively felt that it was the polite and respectful thing to do! She would walk up to a family member who would hug her, pet her, etc. Then she would walk over to someone else and the same greeting would take place. Normally she would then come to wherever I was sitting and just lie down, not moving again until it was time to go. If the patient wanted to see her for any extended period of time during the visit she would go over and lay down by him. For those of you who understand the power of canine presence, picturing the comfort this would bring is an easy thing.

When it came time to leave I would stand up, and by now I'm betting you can guess what happens next. Eclipse would repeat her greeting ceremony, going to each person to say good-bye. Somehow she never missed anyone. To this day I cannot figure out how she figured out the polite thing to do upon leaving. After the last person was finished saying good-bye to her, she would calmly walk over to my side. With no leash needed, we would head outside, where she would jump into the back of the car with a, "We did good," look on her face. While I'm sure quite a number of people would say a dog can't possibly know about proper greeting procedure, or knowing that she had really made a difference in a family's day, all I can say is, "You had to be there."

The Funeral Mass

After about a year of visits to this family, we were informed by Hospice that the gentleman had passed away. His family had a nice visit, and was just leaving at the time. His daughter was supposed to go on an extended cruise a day or so later, and of course was debating whether or not to go, since she realized that her father was in the final stages of the dying process. They just went out to their car, and when his wife went back in she found her husband had died. Did he choose to leave this world at that particular time, since he had just said good-bye to his family, and this would save them the agony of making a decision about their upcoming trip? If so, it by no means will be the first, or the last time, something like this occurred. Many times in Hospice, patients stay alive while waiting for an out of town family member to arrive, or until a much anticipated wedding, birthday, etc. When my father was on Hospice, my mother refused to leave his side, even for a minute. When a forgotten about appointment with a local physician came up for her, we convinced her to leave the house for just a half hour or so. We received the call that my father had died while we were at the office visit. Could it be that he chose this time to leave the world, to spare the family being there at the moment of death? While we would have liked to have been there, apparently he had other plans. It seems that we have more control over our conditions than we may realize. Good for us!

The family called, to ask if I could come to the wake and funeral mass. As I'm sure you understand by now, the request was really for Eclipse. While she does have a license it does not include driving privileges, so I was of course included in the request. Naturally, having a canine at a funeral mass is not a normal occurrence. The church had a few reservations about it.

Going into the funeral home we were greeted by a mob of people. The deceased was very well known in the area. After going up to the coffin to pay our respects, I knew that just finding a seat would be a problem. While I looked around the room to find a free chair, Eclipse just curled up in front of the coffin. It seemed like she was saying, "This is my friend, and I should lay by him here, just as I did by his chair at his home." At that moment, who should walk in, but the priest that I believe was going to be officiating at the next day's funeral mass. He took one look at Eclipse lying calmly by the deceased, while people were filing by, talking, and basically taking up every bit of space in the room." He came over to me and said, "She can come tomorrow." No doubt he never expected a dog to act the way she did. To be honest with you, if he had said that she would not be welcome, we would still be there. To me, the family's requests beat official rules any time of the day.

The following morning we entered the church, and chose an empty pew. Of course Eclipse simply laid down and never made a sound for the entire mass. On the other side of the church, a friend of mine, who also knew the family, spotted me and came over. Boy, was she surprised when she looked down and saw a dog. At the end of the mass, the casket, with family following, and the priest in front, is wheeled to the front doors. If you can believe it, he actually stopped the procession for a few minutes right in front of us, and gave words of blessing to Eclipse. Religious organizations love the idea of a conversion to their particular spiritual beliefs. It was easy to see that Eclipse had made a convert out of this religious leader, from one dubious about dogs in church, to one that understood their power of emotional healing. Chalk up another one up for my team leader!

A major hospice concept is that the death process is not only about the patient, but is rather is a total family experience. We follow the family for a year or more if they so desire, offering bereavement support, mailings, memorial services, etc. Since the widow in this case was basically living alone at this time, Eclipse continued her visits. I know for certain that she made a difference. After all, this is what therapy dogs are all about. To this day, we continue to maintain contact with the family.

A Chance Encounter

One day we were going into see my mother in the hospital. She had just had successful back surgery to relieve her constant pain. We had just entered, and were about to proceed to her room, when a woman who was leaving the hospital couldn't wait to meet me. Well, something like that. One look at my "magnet" dog and she was pulled to where we were standing. Apparently her husband was in the hospital, and wasn't exactly having a wonderful stay. She mentioned that if at all possible, it would brighten his day if he could meet Eclipse. Seems like they had goldens in the past, and let me tell you, once a golden lover, always a golden lover!

After visiting my mother, we made our way to his room. Have you ever seen a gloomy expression change to one of sheer joy in a millisecond? That's about what happened. The patients name was Robert, and I truly felt like the visit brought some sunlight into his otherwise dismal day. Chalk another one up for Eclipse, therapy dog par excellence!

When leaving the hospital, Mom required extensive physical therapy, which necessitated a rehabilitation facility stay. Eclipse was not only a registered therapy dog, but also a full-fledged volunteer at the facility, which was also a nursing home. When we visited Mom each day, Eclipse was with us....of course.

We were just arriving for the evening, when who should walk out but the woman we met in the hospital lobby a couple of weeks before. What were the odds? She told us she had been trying to find out who we were since she first met us at the hospital. Seems like the next day the first thing that her husband said to her was, "Guess who came to visit me last night?" He had a big smile on his face, and said, "I met Howard." Well, those weren't his exact words. Perhaps they were more along the lines of "I met Eclipse." I'm not sure, but I have a strong sensation that you most certainly are! She asked if we could visit with her husband, and so started a friendship of two families that lasts to this day.

I would see her husband each day when visiting with Mom. When she went back home, and he had to stay, my visits continued. Some days we would talk about very serious issues. At other times the topics would be quite light and totally unmedical. Many times words were not necessary. He would just spend time watching Eclipse lying on the floor. I would watch with him. Two adults spending the better part of an evening watching a golden retriever lying on the floor doing absolutely nothing? High blood pressure, anxiety, discomfort, simple or complex worries, or any similar problems in your life? Get a golden and just watch him or her doing nothing. It works. They have the ability to simply share their peacefulness with those around them. I have a feeling they know our needs, and try to fulfill them. Can an animal really do this? Let me try to expound on the answer in enough detail to scientifically explain it. "YES, they can!"

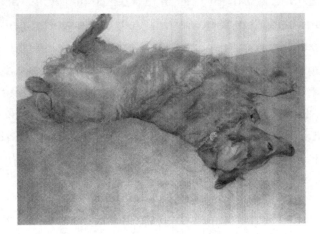

Another Religious Experience

It was a sad day when I received a call stating that our new friend Bob had died. While of course this was expected at some time soon, due to the nature of his disease, it always comes as a shock. People would say it must get easier as a Hospice volunteer to deal with the death of a patient, after being around the dying process for years, and dealing with the death of many patients. As any Hospice volunteer will tell you, the answer is an unequivocal, "NO." These people go very quickly from patients to friends. I have a strong feeling that as soon as a death doesn't affect you much anymore, it's time to find a new area to volunteer in.

There was to be a memorial service at a small community church. One of the widow's major requests was that I attend and be with her during the entire service. For those who have reached this part of the book I'm sure you spot the obvious fallacy in the last sentence. Got it? Sure you do. She wanted Eclipse with her!

Eclipse, my wife, and I, arrived at the church which was totally packed with people. The crowd was spilling out the door. People were forced to stand outside, it was so crowded. Apparently I, correction, Eclipse, was expected, and we were asked to go inside. Now I knew she would be well behaved. That was never even a consideration. However, to this day people that were at the memorial service continue to comment on her demeanor. The widow kept Eclipse by her side at all times, even when she went up for communion. Eclipse and I went up to receive communion with her, and if you can even imagine it, here is a dog, in a packed church, just sitting there looking like she had been in this situation many times. On a funny note, the widow later told me that before the service began she had asked the priest to give a dog biscuit to Eclipse at communion. He declined. I will admit that that could have been pushing the envelope a bit ☺

Picture this. It's the end of the memorial service, and Eclipse is lying in the aisle between the pews. The choir comes down the aisle to sing one final song. They formed a circle around Eclipse, and began singing. Naturally she did not even move a muscle. I don't think I'll ever forget the sight of her being surrounded and serenaded. If my mind ever begins to forget, I'm sure my heart won't.

After the service, a get together was held in the meeting room of the church and food was served. We were invited to join them, and let me tell you this. Since there was food involved, there was no way that Eclipse was going to miss out on it. Naturally she would never take food if it was not offered to her. Trust me when I say that it was offered. Later on in the year we were invited to return to the church for a blessing of the animals, and again you can guess who was invited to stay for snacks.

We have stayed good friends with the man's widow, and have been in her home on several occasions. Each time you could easily see the effect Eclipse had on her. One day when we were visiting her, a reporter from a local newspaper came and did a full page story about Eclipse, and her interactions with the family. So nice for people to read about the role of a therapy dog. Sometime after this the priest actually adopted a golden retriever form LIGRR. My only question is, "Has he reconsidered biscuits for canines at communion?

Hospitals and Therapy Don't Mix

Think of a place where a therapy dog can interact with many sick people, and make their lives better, if only for a little while. If you said," The hospital," you fully agree with me. Now, if the hospital looked at things our way everything would work our perfectly. Unfortunately, this was not the case in my situation.

Many evenings while visiting my mother in the hospital, I would go with Eclipse. Naturally my mother's face brightened when she saw us come in the room. I will use the pronoun, "we," so I can get some of the credit for the reaction, rather than give it all to my canine partner. Quite often another patient would ask to see Eclipse. After checking with the nurse to make sure entering their room was medically sound, we would do what we could to let them forget about their conditions for a little while, and enjoy my partner's company.

One problem always occurred. If I wanted to get to my mother's room at six o'clock, I would have to get to the hospital about an hour early. Getting past the nurse stations was quite difficult. Working a stressful job means that they insisted on their therapy time as well, and would mob Eclipse for a little bit of love. One time, a few medical workers came running down the hall to help with the patient that they thought must have fallen and was in distress. All they saw was a bunch of nurses on the floor surrounding someone. Naturally when they arrived they noticed the someone was Eclipse. The other nurses were simply on the floor with her. Looked good to them, so they joined the crowd.

Hard to tell you how many nurses made comments about the great work that Eclipse was doing and the tremendously positive comments they received from the patients. While it is hard to tell you the number of nurses making positive comments, I can easily tell you the number that made negative ones. The answer is one. You would think that a single negative would have little effect. Think again!

Standing in the hallway, a nurse asked me what the dog was doing there. No problem. I told her that I worked for Hospice, and Eclipse was the official Hospice dog, as well as a registered therapy dog with Therapy Dogs International. While I was explaining this to her, her fellow nurses, who were standing behind her, looked at me, pointed at her, and mouthed the word, "B_ _ _ H." She told me to wait there while she called the nursing supervisor for the hospital.

A minor bump in the road. No Problem. It would only take a few minutes to straighten the situation out. Here it is, years later, and the problem is still not remedied. The nursing supervisor was very cooperative. She said that she thought therapy dogs were wonderful, but to keep everyone happy she asked us to not visit anymore that day. She would contact hospital administration, and all would be taken care of after an official ruling was given. What could possibly happen? I had been a hospice volunteer for over fifteen years; Eclipse was the official Hospice dog, as well as being a registered therapy dog. What could possibly happen? Stupidity and a lack of even considering for a moment the wellbeing of patients! That's what could happen. Meeting with the head of Hospice, I was informed that the hospital's lawyers had reviewed policy. There was nothing one way or the other about therapy dogs. Therefore, "to play it safe," they decided that she was not allowed in the hospital. In other words, let's protect ourselves, and the heck with the patients. Such a simple legal judgment, and such a disgrace to the Hospice philosophy!

A decision was later made to form a committee to draft a possible therapy dog policy. Of course I was not invited to join, since that would probably have made sense. After many months they arrived at some discussion points. Bureaucracy at its best. I saw the long list of things they were considering. My favorite was, "Should the dog be required to use the stairs or the elevator?" I suppose that's why I never went into administration. Having to make such life altering decisions would have gotten to me. Here it is a few years later and no definitive policy is in place, and patients are being denied the benefits of a Hospice therapy dog.

Ready for a final laugh? Being ill myself, and forbidden by physicians to go into hospitals or nursing homes, etc., due to a weakened immune system, I have not been that actively involved in hospice for a year or so. While Eclipse does have a license, it does not entitle her to driving privileges, and so by extension she could not visit patient's homes without my driving skills. Made me feel kind of important! I did get one bit of news recently that initially made me quite upset, but now just gives me a laugh the more I think about it.

Eclipse was always the only registered therapy dog working with Hospice. Speaking with a staff member recently, I found out that while therapy dogs are still not allowed in the hospital, they are allowed to make home visits. After the whole hospital decision, patients were obligated to sign wavers if they wanted a canine visit, but I had no problems with that. Therapy dogs registered with Therapy Dogs international are insured for liability up to one million dollars, should an incident arise that might cause injuries, etc. to a patient. Probably never needed, but nice to have. Somehow I sincerely doubt if the new Hospice therapy dogs are equally insured. While I have been recently informed that no visits have ever taken place, allow me to tell you about Eclipse's replacements. Let me give you a few minutes to let you guess the answer to the following question. What would be the most ironic attribute of the new dogs being used? You can even refer back to a previous chapter and it wouldn't be cheating. Give up? Here's a hint for you. Eclipse couldn't work for them. Yup, the vet who declared Eclipse to have a bad temperament, and not even to be worthy of training, now has his people involved. While I certainly believe patients will benefit from the visiting dogs, a part of me still says, "You got to be kidding." Apparently not.

Mom's Little Helper

If you remember, one of the main reasons I was not really into getting another dog was that my mother was getting on in years, and a canine would present two problems. The first one was that even though my mother lived next door, we knew as time went by, she would require more assistance, and more of our time. While being fiercely independent, I'm sure she wouldn't have agreed, but we kind of knew it.

Since moving in next door about thirty years before, my parents had always taken care of our dogs when we would be on a vacation, or were just out for more than a few hours. There was no way my mother was going to give up this job. Severe back and neck pain, and any other physical problems she might have had were not going to deter her. This we knew for a fact. In case you are wondering why we couldn't just tell her not to get so involved taking care of a new dog, about all I can say is, "You didn't know my mother." As far as she was concerned, taking care of us, and helping (and feeding) people in need were her reasons for living.

Let's just say Eclipse proved me totally wrong about the effect she would have, in terms of us being able to care for my mother. She made the job a lot easier than it would have been, had she not entered our lives.

From day one my mother adored her, and the feeling was mutual. It was truly a "grandogta" "grandmutter" relationship. Silly? Believe it or not when my father was alive we always referred to him as "grandpaw". Yeah, I know. We're a little strange, but hopefully in a good way.

Unfortunately my mother started having some major medical problems right after Eclipse joined the family. She always had arthritis, some heart problems, and back pain; even a bout with shingles. This is a particularly unpleasant disease. If you have ever had the chicken pox, you have the shingles virus in you, which can rear its ugly head at any time. The pain involved can be quite intense! Mom also started to experience some mental deterioration which she just about refused to accept. This refusal is very natural for a person who dedicated her life to helping others. She always handled her own affairs. She even drove a car until she was about ninety years old. To even admit that things were starting to mess up a bit, was just not in her realm of believable possibilities.

As previously mentioned, at one point Mom needed back surgery to relieve some of the constant pain that she experienced. While the surgery went well, and certainly helped with the pain issues, she was in the hospital for a while, and then spent some time in a rehabilitation setting. Mom could accept the hospital as necessary, but the idea of a "nursing home/rehab," facility went against everything she stood for. Which was, basically, that home is where she belonged. While certainly agreeing with her, we also understood that there was absolutely no way to give her proper care at home. Calling in a few favors we were able to get her into the best rehab/nursing home in town. We did have a family member who worked at this facility, and was considered an integral staff member, loved by all of the residents, and whose talents were considered essential in helping to make life in the facility better. Nope, not me. Yes, Eclipse. Saw that one coming didn't you.

Of course visiting with Mom each day meant planning to spend a couple additional hours visiting with other patients, as well as giving the staff their obligatory therapy visits. One of our favorite patients was a one hundred and five year old lady who was blind and just about deaf. I always remember the first time I went into her room. Screaming into her ear, I told her a dog was here to see her. The nurses told me she loved animals. Her first question was, "What's the dog's name?" I told her and she said, "That's a crappy name." When you get to be over a hundred years old you can express any opinions you might have, and this fantastic lady was noted for expressing them. Eclipse would lay by her chair so the woman could "Braille" her for the whole visit. Beautiful to see! We would even go into rooms where a patient might be considered uncommunicative. We'd walk in, sit down, and many times a conversation would ensue. Between the patient and Eclipse, of course. More than one patient has made the statement that, "Today has been a bad day, but it isn't anymore." That's a therapy dog team's reason for being!

I don't have to tell you that having Eclipse around helped Mom to better accept the situation. The decision was made by all concerned, minus Mom of course, that upon returning home she had to have someone with her at all times to take care of such chores as food preparation, help getting around, and other activities of daily living. We went with the most highly recommended agency to find the correct person. There would be one lady who would live with my mother twenty four hours a day during the week, who would then be replaced on weekends by someone else.

Let me begin by saying that the aide was excellent. We couldn't have asked for anyone better. Unfortunately things started off poorly, and then went downhill from there. The head of the agency came with the aide on day one to explain her duties, and more or less left my mother out of the discussion. Not a particularly good move. Here's Mom, in her home/castle, with no input. Not a nice scenario. The agency head leaves. We decide to go home (remember, we only live next door) and see what would develop. It developed in about a half hour.

Eclipse is Now the Favorite

Our phone rings. It's Mom saying we better get over there because the aide is following her around everywhere she goes. While this seems like just perfect, caring behavior for a caregiver, let's just say Mom didn't view it quite that way. I explained to all of her aides that there were a few dozen things that Mom was not supposed to do, but that I would not be telling them what they were, since she would be doing them anyway. I urged them to just "be there," and that I understood that anything that happened to Mom was not their fault. This worked a little bit better, but naturally the whole setup wasn't Mom's idea of the way things were supposed to be. On a funny side note, I think Mom's favorite, let's change that to least hated aide, was a girl that came on weekends. She followed my instructions to a tee, and basically just sat and read to herself all weekend.

Of course we were over at Mom's every day to listen to her complaints about the aides, etc. Believe me; things would have been so much worse had it not been for the great calming influence of Eclipse. As soon as we entered Mom's home, her eyes would open wide and her previously wide smile would appear when she saw her "grandogta".

She would always have some small treats and one by one would feed her best friend. More treats served one at a time ended the evening. To Eclipse, there was never anything more wonderful than food, and she would just sit in front of Mom and wait for the treats to be slowly dispensed. We never worried about her jumping on Mom or grabbing for a treat. Just not in her respectful nature. At this point Mom still loved us, but with the aide and all, Eclipse was moving up rapidly into the number one position. We certainly understood this. Without her calming nature, which somehow calmed everyone around her, things could have been so much worse. We finally made a deal with Mom to slowly phase out the aides. Joy reigned temporarily in Mudville.

Eclipse Continues to Do Her Work

Some months went by, and while Mom's back surgery did take away a lot of the pain, she still was quite compromised, and her speech problems were progressing. As my wife would say, "She just doesn't seem to be Mom anymore." I mentioned this to someone and loved their response, "It is Mom, just Mom at this point in her life." How true! My mother never had a bad word to say about anybody. She accepted whatever came along without complaint, and lived to help others. Not being able to move about, and conduct business as usual was just unacceptable to her. I'm pretty sure she realized that things were starting to scramble up a bit, but not to the extent that they were. We took her to many doctors and a diagnosis of severe dementia was finally made when we found a very compassionate geriatric neuropsychiatrist. Other doctors just described her problems as social ones. One doctor just asked me, "Are you the same as you were thirty years ago?" After a while you start to question your ideas and decisions.

Naturally, visiting the physicians was not something that we could accomplish without much protest. One thing did help. Yup, Eclipse. Mom knew that a trip to the doctors would include her friend. She would like to be in the waiting room telling others about this wonderful dog, who just laid there by her feet. When it came our turn to see the doctor, Eclipse would continue to lay by Mom's feet. Somehow she just knew were the calming energy was needed most. When possible, we would stop at Starbucks on the way home, so Mom could get her Venti half caff, soy, white chocolate mocha, no whip no foam. Try it, you'll like it! At her feet would be Eclipse of course. I really don't like to think of what the physician visits would have been like if Eclipse's calming energy was not present.

Several months later Mom was back in the hospital with back and other problems. There was no way she could return home without twenty-four hour assistance. An aide I was familiar with from my Hospice work had just become available. I knew she was the best, so naturally we asked her to take care of Mom. While the aide tried her best, Mom naturally objected to having someone take over her home. I could certainly understand her feelings. She did however realize that there was no way she could live alone. It was to be a very tough year for all concerned. Except of course for Eclipse. Besides daytime visits, we went over to see my mother every evening. To say that Eclipse was the hit of each visit was to put it mildly. Mom's face lit up, and the treats came out. Much of the evening was spent talking about Eclipse's activities in Hospice, etc. While she certainly was a calming influence on Mom, it must be noted that our lives during this difficult time would have been unbearably stressful had Eclipse not been around. Just "being around," reduced the stress for us. Talk about a therapy dog. The hours of calming therapy that she gave to us was so very instrumental in our being able to better take care of my mother.

More Health Problems, and More Help from Eclipse

About a year or so later Mom broke her hip and wound up in a nursing home. It was the same facility where she had previously been for therapy. We kept her aide with her, but Mom's desire to keep going was just gone. We went each day, with Eclipse of course, who would lay by her bed after receiving her treats, for as long as we were there. Since she was an "official" therapy dog of the facility, she was welcomed at all times.

One instance always comes to mind. One night my mother was being examined by a nurse and a doctor, who spent about twenty minutes with her. Just as they were about to leave the nurse said to the doctor, "Some quiet dog isn't it?" The doctor gave her a funny look and said, "There's a dog in here?" He really never spotted her laying there. As I mentioned, all hell could be breaking loose, and she would just calmly stay where she was. Sometimes it was downright spooky. It was a linoleum tiled room, so if Eclipse was laying somewhere where a nurse had to get to, rather than have her get up, we simply would slide her out of the way. Eclipse, not the nurse!

About a month or so later, my mother, while staying in the facility, became enrolled in the Hospice program where she, my wife and I volunteered. At this point she was having a lot of problems, but I swear I never saw such a smile on her face as when she realized she was going to be a part of this program. Many people might think of Hospice as giving up. It is not! It's simply living the rest of your life without annoying medical procedures, while at the same time receiving proper medication to keep yourself pain free, yet as full a part of life as possible. Not a bad set of desires for anyone, is it?

The Midnight Call

A few weeks later I received a call near midnight informing me that Mom was showing signs of being close to death. While knowing she had really wanted this time to come, once she no longer saw a purpose in her life, made it a bit easier for me, but you can easily guess my feelings at that moment. Pick an emotion! I was feeling it. Within a few minutes I was in the car, and on my way. Arriving fifteen minutes later, I was met at the door, and told that Mom had passed away. I went to her room, gave her a kiss, told her I loved her, and a whole bunch of other things about how I felt. Then I simply sat by the bed for some time. It was now about two in the morning and I called my wife. After telling her what happened, I asked her to drive in and be with me. Sort of. All I can remember about the call was asking her to bring Eclipse to me. Perhaps a strange request, but so be it.

My wife shows up a little while later with my friend. Eclipse comes over to me and gives me a look that said more than any person could have said to comfort me. After looking at me and Mom for a minute or so, she simple laid down next to the bed, as if to say, "I'm here. " For those of you who have lost a loved one, a friend who is simply there with you, is something that I'm sure you cherish more than anything else. Words can be empty. Feelings cannot.

At the funeral home, you just know that Eclipse was there at all times. She would lay by the coffin, or follow me around as I talked to people. One thing I will never forget. On the final evening of the wake, Eclipse's minister got up to speak. Yup, Eclipse's. Remember the memorial service I described where the choir sang around her? While we did not belong to that church, it always seemed like Eclipse did. The priest from that church was now officiating. Certainly seemed fitting. I took my seat in the front row, and Eclipse came from the side of the room. She sat, pushing into me, as if to say, "I'm here for you," and stayed there for the whole service.

If you remember, a couple of years before I did not want a dog due to the fact that my mother needed care, and a dog would just complicate matters in so many ways. I've been wrong before, but happily never as wrong as I was about that. Without Eclipse's calming energy, I sometimes wonder how our family could have gotten through this difficult time in our lives. Someone once asked if we received professional counseling to assist us. I simply said, "Of course we did, and we had the best!"

LIGRR

After doing a few fund raisers with the rescue group, I slowly became more and more involved. After a couple years of helping out, I was asked to be on the board. It made me very proud to be asked. Of course I accepted. My salary and compensation was to be double that of the group's president! Wait a minute. Two times zero is not all that much!

My desire to become more actively involved hinged on two major factors. One was obviously due to my love of Golden Retrievers. They are such wonderful animals who at times need special assistance. Since they cannot handle problems on their own, this is where we, as animal lovers, must step forward.

My second reason for getting more involved came as a result of seeing what Long Island Golden Retriever Rescue (LIGRR) was all about, and getting to know its volunteers, who to this day amaze me at the effort they are willing to put out in helping these amazing canines. Absolutely no one in the group receives even a penny in salary, compensation, etc. Don't for a minute think that means they break even at the end of the year. Many times they will spend their own funds to help wherever needed. They transport animals to veterinary hospitals, and foster sick animals to see them through to a point where they can be adopted. They evaluate a dog's behavior so proper placement can be made, do home visits to prospective adopters so that a good match occurs, and spend many hours standing in the cold selling raffle tickets, etc. Basically they will do anything they are called upon to do. Believe me; they do it with smiles on their faces!

LIGRR is considered a non-profit organization. It does not have a shelter. Dogs stay with volunteers, live in foster homes, or stay with their present owners until a forever family is found. In a worst case scenario the dog is boarded in a veterinarian's office. Bad for the dog, and certainly for our bottom line.

If only LIGRR broke even at the end of the year. The organization is always "in the red." They take in any dog, regardless of age or medical condition. As I'm writing this we just took in a young dog that is going to require about ten thousand dollars in surgery. Never a question about whether we would take him. A thirteen year old senior with severe issues? He becomes ours. I'm sure you can see how the bills come rolling in.

Once a dog is taken in by LIGRR he is set for life. If a new owner wants to get rid of a dog we have placed with them, the requirement is simply that it must be returned to us. I have seen dogs that were abandoned, or simply found wandering the streets. Some of them in terrible shape. All I can think about once they are accepted by the group is, "Now you are safe, and will be forever." Right there, is reason enough to do the job that we do!

I would urge you to check us out at LIGRR.org. On our web-site you can lean more of what we are all about. Of course while you are there my hope is that you will make a small (or large☺) donation. Know that one hundred percent of anything you donate will "go to the dogs." Not many groups can make that claim. With absolutely no one in the group receiving a penny, we can honestly say that. If you would like to donate in Eclipse's memory, that would be wonderful. Thanks in advance.

Enter Mozart

When we first found out that Eclipse was going to be placed with us, we were given the option of fostering her until the surgery was completed, and then adopting her. If we did foster her, it was for about thirty seconds. I guess that qualified us for what the rescue group calls "foster failure," status. You take care of a dog, and when it's time for the animal to get adopted you have come to love it so much, that it becomes a member of your family. Happens quite a bit.

Now we were happy with just having Eclipse. My wife and I never had two dogs at the same time, and when you have an animal like her why would you want to mess with perfection?

There was a dog, Mozart, that originally lived in California. His original owner came to New York, but had to go to Europe. Rather than have the dog quarantined for an extended time overseas, he surrendered him. LIGRR found him a great home. For the next seven years or so he led a nice life in Brooklyn, NY, with a fine family. Through a series of events the family had a breakup. The man that adopted him had a new wife of a year or so, as well as a young daughter from his previous marriage.

The new owner served overseas, and tragically, on his way back to the states, dies of a heart attack. Here is his new family in a state of shock. The new wife must now return to work, and in her words, "The dog has to go." Once a dog is in our program we are obligated to take him back, no questions asked.

My wife and I were to meet the family from Brooklyn, halfway between where they lived and our home, a distance of about forty miles for both of us. We were to meet at a gas station on the side of the Long Island Expressway.

When we arrived, I notice that the station was closed for repairs, but did see two things. One was a parked car. The other was a rather large golden retriever. He was properly labeled. Here were three gas pumps; Regular, Special, and Super. This dog was lying there, right by the Super pump!

One of the station attendants insisted that we leave since the place was officially closed. We followed the family down the road to a small parking area. They were very nice and you could see they cared very much for the dog, but were just unable to keep it. We loaded him into the back of our car, along with all his toys, bed, etc. We assured the family that Mozart would receive any medical treatment needed, and that we could guarantee that he would be placed with a loving family. It's hard for people to give up an animal they love. We, as a rescue group, can ease the pain a bit, by letting them know that their animal will be well taken care of for the rest of its life.

All the way home he just laid there and looked at us. Sort of reminded me of another dog a couple of years before? We stopped at a vet on the way home to get him checked out.

He had many lumps on him, some bad teeth, and an infection or something going on by one of his front feet. LIGRR would of course take care of the medical, and we would take care of Mozart.

Arriving home we had a meet and greet with Eclipse. As predicted, all went fine. Well, Mozart....Welcome to the pack: temporarily of course. So I thought at the time. His previous owners mentioned that he slept in the "sitting room" at night. About an hour after arriving home we look in the living room and there he is lying stretched out on the couch. Not ridiculous, but lying on the floor stretched out against the couch was Eclipse. It was almost as if she was saying to him, "I'm sure you are a little confused by all the things that happened today, but know that I am here for you." If any dog could and would say this to another animal, it would, without a doubt, be Eclipse!

As he recovered from his surgeries, all was going well. According to his intake form he didn't like people touching his foot. I had to soak it each day, and after learning that handing over your foot, results in kibble going into your mouth, we had no problems. Most amazing dog I've ever seen in terms of gently taking food. If you offered him something to eat, all you had to do was hold out your hand. He would come over and basically "kiss" the item, and let it fall into his mouth. Most gentle dog in this respect that I have ever seen! Don't get me wrong. Eclipse was gentle also, but when your jaw is swinging back and forth it's hard to take food normally. We had a Toyota Prius and another car even smaller. Wherever we went the boy and girl came along. Looked sort of like one of those circus cars, where they stuff all the clowns inside. The two of them loved to be in the car, since it meant being with their family, and were very content to just chill out, and enjoy the ride. Even if I parked for an hour or more they just slept, while I might read a book in the front seat. Was always fun to have them with us, and of course a source of joy for anyone we met.

Another Failure

About a week after getting Mozart, we were scheduled to go away for ten days, on our first real vacation in quite a long time. We boarded the new guy on the block in the kennel that we always used, and things worked out pretty well. Naturally Eclipse came with us.

Two or three months later, with the boy fully recovered, it was time for him to find his forever home. As you can guess, he had already found it! We just couldn't bear to let him go. When you help a dog through the rough times you just form a special bond. With Mozart I think we bonded on the way home with him from meeting his former family at the gas station. Here we were, a "Foster Failure," once again,... and proud of it.

Mozart proved to be a wonderful addition to the pack. He interacted beautifully with Eclipse. While they might go their separate ways at times, at other times they would be laying there in a pile. You could just sit and watch them lay there for the longest time. So restful for the mind. They got along so well, and never had any problems. For instance, he loved toys, and Eclipse had no use for them. He would be playing with one, and she would come over, look at him, and had a look that sort of said, "You can't eat those, you know."

Eclipse taught him the important things about being a member of the pack. For instance, when they were first let out in the morning, Eclipse would quickly run back to the house. She couldn't wait to get in and get her breakfast. Mozart would meander around while she waited by the porch door,.....Impatiently! But only for a short amount of time. Then she would go over to where he was, look him in the face as if to say, "it's food time."Then they would both go in. She'd let him in the porch first, but would bump him out of the way to get in the main door first. Hey, love for your brother is one thing, but love for you breakfast supersedes it! A little while after they ate, my wife would have her breakfast on the porch. She would share breakfast with them, which was the only "people food," we ever gave them. When he first arrived he would eat his regular breakfast, and then go back to bed. We had to teach him to go out to the porch for breakfast sharing. While Eclipse taught him a lot of things, going to have this second breakfast wasn't one of them. I wonder why? ☺

She helped him in so many ways. He was a more nervous dog, and would be afraid of fireworks, thunderstorms and the like. I swear that he would get a bit excited, but before it escalated he would look at Eclipse, who might be resting on the cold tiles, or upside down against a wall. I'm sure her thoughts that she transmitted to him were something like, "Don't sweat it. It's no big deal." He generally got the message.

She even taught him tolerance. According to his intake forms he was very possessive of his bed. About a week after he arrived on the scene, I bought a nice new orthopedic one for him. I showed him the receipt, and told him it was my bed, but he could use it. This plus a little additional training with treats pretty much took care of things. I knew all was well one day when he goes to his bed and sees Eclipse laying in it. She normally never does this, and he never goes in hers. For a minute or two they just looked at each other. It's like Mozart was saying, "My bed, My bed, Nobody goes in my bed." Eclipse's response was probably something in the order of, "So use mine. It's really no big deal." He turned around and walked away.

When you would give them treats or when my wife fed them some of her breakfast they would sit squashed up against each other, with their heads just about touching. Here's two food crazed dogs, and never once did they give the other the evil eye, or try to grab the other's food. Guess they just respected each other, and maybe had even read Emily Post's book on table manners. Never actually saw them reading it, but with those two, you never knew!

We even took him on a couple of Hospice visits, so he could learn from the best. While he wasn't a certified therapy dog or anything, we did have Eclipse's "training vest," so I might have cheated a little. One incident did occur at a nursing home that we got the biggest kick out of!

We visited a patient who had gout of the foot. Mozart goes over to her; puts his head on the bad foot, and leaves it there for the whole visit. A natural! On the way in and out he met and said hello to many other patients. While Eclipse wasn't a "licker," Mozart loved to give each new person he met a "kiss," on the nose. All of a sudden he pulls quite hard on his leash. He was intent on getting over to one particular person across the room. Did he sense that she needed his newfound therapeutic abilities? No. You see she was using a walker, and many times items are used on the legs of the walker to make them slide easier on the floor. What's used as the "sliders?" Tennis balls of course. Mozart's favorite thing in the whole world. So funny!

We were extremely happy that we failed in successfully fostering him. He became a wonderful member of the pack, and a terrific brother for Eclipse.

Amyloi What ??

During the last few months of my mother's life I had been feeling a little short of breath. No big deal, since stress is not exactly good for one's health. Problem was that the symptoms never seemed to go away, even after life sort of returned to normal. Then the saga began.

Having a regular checkup a few months later my family physician felt it was time for my every so many year nuclear stress test. No big deal. As those of you who have had one of these know, you are injected with radioactive something or other, a scan is done, you get hooked up with a dozen or so electrical leads and step on the treadmill. To me all of this was probably why they called it a "stess test!" My speed etc., wasn't what it used to be (I used to run marathons a few years back).

My physician noted a couple of things, but there didn't seem to be anything too troubling. Of course the results had to be completely analyzed. I received a call saying that things looked pretty good, but just to be sure I should see a cardiologist.

I was referred to a well-known, top of the line specialist. My appointment wasn't for a couple of weeks, so no big deal. The result of that checkup was that I should have a cardiac catheterization. If you have ever had one you know that physically there is no great discomfort. However, mentally thinking about some camera being inserted into your crotch and led up into your heart seems mighty wrong! As I was being wheeled into the room for the procedure, the doctor gave me good news. He said that based upon the echocardiogram that he took in his office the week before, he doubted very much that I had any blockages. Great news! Being just about a complete vegan for many years, I kind of assumed this. Of course what he said next was interesting. I still remember his words. "This is just the tip of the iceberg." Unfortunately truer words were never spoken. After the procedure he said he was sending me for an MRI before I left the hospital, and then asked me if I had an oncologist. Cardiac catheterization, and then a referral to an oncologist? Somehow the two didn't seem to go together.

Many years in the past I did have a single consultation with an oncologist who I always remembered as such a caring person. Here it is ten years later and I'm going back to see him. He is just about the top hematologist/oncologist on Long island, and to put it mildly, he is still the same caring person I remembered him to be. When you are with him, you are the only patient in the world, and never feel rushed. You get whatever exam time you need or want. A real gem!

A couple of months later based upon his testing and a stomach fat pad biopsy (seems unrelated…no?), I was diagnosed with a disease called Amyloidosis. Let's put it this way. If you received a list of all the diseases in the world you could come up with, this is not only by far one of the rarest, but also one of the, "I hope I never get that one, " diseases. No known cause or cure.

The disease is what it is, and I'm receiving better medical care than 99.999% of the world could hope to receive, from a dedicated team of caring, top of their fields, medical personnel. The top cardiologist. An oncologist in NYC who specializes in the disease, and my local, best of the best oncologist. Along with them is my primary care physician. He is the type of physician that is always willing to go the extra mile, or two, when you need him. Beyond their obvious medical excellence, they are all great human beings. To me this is oh so important. In other words, no complaints in the slightest. Plus, this book is about Eclipse, not me, so not to worry. You won't have to hear all the medical details. I only mentioned my illness to set the stage for the continued amazing behavior of my "heart dog."

TD to RN

It always struck me as rather nice that Eclipse was so happy and contented to be with her family. We weren't "joined at the hip," but she was never far away from where I was in the house, or if we were out at a fund raiser, etc. No doubt due to the fact that we trained together for therapy work, went everywhere together from visiting Hospice and nursing home patients, to fund raising etc. The two of us sort of had this "communication" thing going on. Almost as if, without words being exchanged, we just somehow knew what the other needed at any particular time.

Eclipse was always a tremendous therapy dog. When people would ask who she does the most therapy for I would always reply, "Me." Just being around her brought me such peace and joy, that little could bother me. Her aura simply said, "Live each moment fully!"

As soon as I was officially diagnosed with Amyloidosis, reports were naturally sent to all of my physicians. Somehow Eclipse must have received a copy. Some kind of change came over her. They say that dogs can sense medical conditions in humans. Work is even being done where dogs are able to tell if a patient has cancer.

This before medical science knows for sure. Call it instinct, refined sense of smell, or whatever you like. It exists, as I was to find out.

As I said, we were generally together, but quite often she would be in another room, sleeping on her bed, laying in the kitchen or bathroom on the tiles (she loved it where it was cool.) After my diagnosis, things changed. I was literally never out of her sight. I couldn't really get out of bed, and she would lay under a small tray table by my bedside. A Chihuahua might have fit pretty well, but not an eighty something pound dog. Somehow she did. If I moved somewhere, she moved, always keeping me in her sight. Many times she wouldn't even move her body, just her eyes. I seriously don't believe I was ever out of her sight! After a couple of months I purchased one of those lift chairs that recline at the push of a button. We put it in the living room, and I spent a lot of the day there, and then used it for sleeping at night. Eclipse wouldn't use her bed that was on the floor in the bedroom. She would lay right next to my chair and hardly change her position. Overnight she might move a few feet away at times, but always in a position to keep her eyes on me. When I wrote the last sentence it made me laugh. She loved to lie upside down against a wall. I guess you would have to say that at times she kept her eyes on me, but they might be upside down! If I had to use the bathroom overnight, I would find her in the hall outside the door, where she would escort me back to my chair. Felt like I had a full time nurse watching out for me 24/7.

Anytime, day or night I could look at Eclipse, and I swear she sent tons of calming energy in my direction. It sure worked. Stress just left me, and somehow just having her there gave me a feeling of peace and security. I have a bracelet that I wear. Engraved on it are the simple words, "It is what it is." This thought seemed like a major part of Eclipse's philosophy. I could spend hours just watching her watching me. Better therapy than any professional could ever give me. Then again she was a registered therapy dog. Or should I say registered nurse?

Calm vs. Comatose

I actually wrote the chapter that follows before this one. It will give some concrete examples of how calm Eclipse really was. After reading it myself I had one thought. "People are going to think this dog is either comatose, or suffers from some physical problems, which prevent her from acting "normal." Nothing could be further from the truth. So, before we get into the calmness factor, let me give you some concrete examples of her "normalness."

A few weeks after she came to us we decided to take her down to the beach. As soon as her feet touched the sand a different dog emerged. She was on a long lead, and basically ran back and forth to the end of the leash. She then proceeds to run huge circles at Olympic winning speed. We were amazed. Another time we took our Jeep out on the beach, and walked her down to where the ocean met the sand. When arriving at the water's edge, Eclipse digs a huge hole in the sand, at an unbelievable pace. She then lies in the hole. The next wave comes in and fills in the hole with her in it. She then gets up and digs another one, gets in it, and waits for the next wave. She was having a ball!

Most of the time in our yard Eclipse just calmly walked around, took care of things, and came back in (a treat awaited her inside.) Every so often she would run around the outside of the yard at record breaking speed. We were even worried she might hurt herself, since she ran so fast, and seemed oblivious to anything in her way. At the end of the run she sometimes proceeded to rapidly dig a hole to China! You could get her to perform this speed/digging demonstration by running around yourself, or just wait for what I guess she felt were the perfect conditions, where she would initiate the behavior all by herself.

I was helping someone train their young two year old golden. A couple of times Eclipse came along, so the youngster could see perfection in action. After some training we put both dogs in the yard. They start to run around at breakneck speed. Who is going fastest? Eclipse! When they would arrive at a bush the younger dog would run around it, while my girl would go right through it! At one point, she was running at full speed, and gets tangled up in one of those metal tomato cages. What does she do? She continues running with the cage wrapped around her head. You had to see it to believe it.

Another time we were walking both dogs in the street. Somehow they both get loose, and proceed to run amok through the neighborhood. Naturally Eclipse returned to me when done demonstrating insane behavior to her young friend.

She didn't demonstrate this "normal," dog behavior too often, but when she did, it was something to see! Does prove she could be a wild one if she chose to be. I guess she knew this too, but also knew her role in life was to give off calming energy to the world.

Examples

I know that I keep stressing how calm Eclipse was. Below you will find just some examples to prove my point. Don't for a minute think she was just scared or submissive. She wasn't either. She simply approached life with this calm aura.

I suppose that one of the first indications of her calmness came the second day we had her. We went up to a local shopping center to walk her around. I was curious about how she would be with strangers. At one point a woman comes up behind her as we are walking, wraps her arms around her, and hugs like crazy. Let me tell you that there are not many dogs out there that would allow such a thing. Eclipse had no real reaction.

The first year we had Eclipse, the fourth of July was approaching. Not a dog's favorite time of year. All my previous dogs hid and shook and tried to get in the bathtub, hid under cabinets, etc. Our block rivals the NYC Macy's fireworks show. You can actually feel the sound on your body. I'm sure she could to, but there was absolutely no reaction from her.

She liked to lay on the cold tiles right inside the front door. If someone would ring the bell, I could literally slide her over a bit, and open the door. The guest could then step over her. During all of this she would rarely move a muscle.

We had a small open boat (a skiff). We would take it to a local boat ramp. The ramps were narrow, and four boats at a time could be launched. From the first time we took her with us, Eclipse would simply lie on the narrow dock, and wait until we asked her to get into the boat. People could step over her. Splashing of water, etc., would take place, and she would just relax there. Here's a golden retriever a few inches from the water showing no indication of jumping in. Naturally, once in the boat she just relaxed by my feet. Once, another boater was stuck out on the water, and we stopped to give him a ride back to the dock. He jumps into our boat and Eclipse pays him no attention whatsoever.

We go to a bereavement camp to be with children who have lost loved ones. At one point, Eclipse is laying on her side, resting. She is surrounded by no less than ten kids. They are holding her legs, paws, ears, tail, while petting her, etc. At one point she got so stressed out that I think her eyes opened slightly ☺ But that's about it.

She was just as calm with other animals. When the rescue group would do fund raising outside of a Petco, Eclipse was the official dog greeter. Got along with every other animal. When we first got her she was laying on our front porch. Along comes a neighborhood cat. It comes up on the porch; looks Eclipse in the eyes, and proceeds to lay down by her. No problems whatsoever.

A junior high school conducts a yearly fund raiser for LIGRR each year. When school was over for the day, my wife, Eclipse, and myself head in. At one point Eclipse is resting on the floor, on her side. She is literally surrounded by a dozen screaming kids, many of them taking flash pictures of her, while lifting her head up, petting her, etc. As time went on there were probably fifty kids that were fawning over her. Her reaction? None. After about a half hour we left. Why? The noise and confusion were driving me crazy. Any more of it and I would have probably bit someone! I'm not so sure if Therapy Dog's International's million dollar liability policy would have covered my attack. Had to get out of there, so I woke up Eclipse and home we went.

One day, during a fund raiser outside of a Petco, one teenager comes along, takes a look at

Eclipse laying there with commotion all around, and seriously asks, "Is she alive?"

In the yard behind ours, there are several pit bulls that are left out most of the time. They bash against our fence, bark, and seem like they would like to have Eclipse and Mozart for dinner. Of course I don't blame them for their behavior. They are left alone and untrained. Any dog might act the same. While Mozart has issues with them, Eclipse would walk calmly around the yard, sometimes coming within a few feet of the fence. She acted as if they weren't even there. I never could get over this. It's almost like she was saying, "I'm no threat, so why would they want to harm me?"

A hurricane was heading our way and we evacuated to a friend's home. Eclipse and Mozart just settled in, and caused no problems whatsoever. It's like they understood the seriousness of the situation, and knew they needed to help out in their own way. I slept on a chair in the living room, while my wife was on a couch. Come morning, we awake to find Eclipse next to my chair (no surprise), and Mozart on the other couch. What's a little hurricane among friends?

So what great principle is illustrated by the above? The way I look at it, Eclipse simply knew that we would take care of things and wouldn't let anything harm her. The boater, fireworks, etc., were being handled by us, and were not of her concern. Many times in life we get so involved in everything! Perhaps we should learn to concern ourselves with things that really matter, and that we have control over, rather than things beyond our control. It's also a good idea to find people we trust, and to in turn trust that they will take care of certain things for us. Frees us up to take care of other important things. (Like eating and sleeping and pooping?)

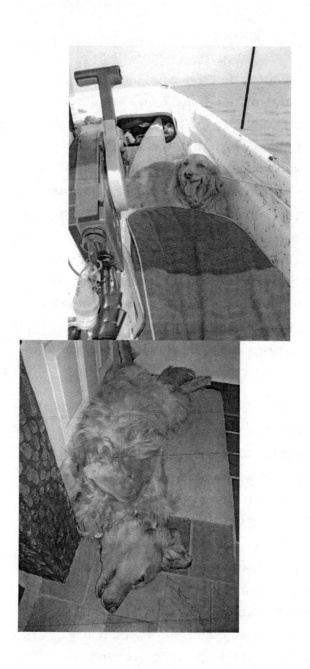

Passing the Torch

I am about to describe what happened during the early summer of 2012. You can draw your own conclusions. At the time, it just stuck me as unusual, but not as anything amazing. Looking back now, I can only come up with one simply amazing explanation for it! Many will say I'm crazy, but then again I've been called worse. Many will say my explanation is ridiculous. I ask you to do two things. One is to allow the fact that I may just be right. Number two? If you think my explanation is just too far out there, I challenge you to come up with a more plausible theory of what happened. I think that you are going to be very hard pressed to do so.

Normally, after going out for the last time at night, Eclipse would take her position by my lift chair in the living room where I slept, and Mozart would go into the bedroom to his bed, which he loved tremendously. One night, an unusual thing occurred. For some reason Mozart showed up in the living room for a half hour or so at the beginning of the night, before going into the bedroom for the remainder of the time. Each evening from that point on he would show up for a little bit longer. My wife and I never could figure out what to make of this behavior. A couple of weeks after he started showing up, I woke during the night and noticed that he was next to my chair. Eclipse was a few feet away looking in our direction.

Now one thing was never debated between them. If Mozart came too close to me, Eclipse would gently push him out of the way. It was as if she were saying, "He's mine." Mozart always moved away. Obviously some canine form of communication was taking place. She never came between us in any sort of upset state, and he never moved aside with any agitation. It was just one of those things that they both understood to be the way it's supposed to be. To see her a few feet away, and him next to my chair might seem like no big deal to you, but to us it was about as strange as things could get. For the next few weeks his time sleeping in the living room increased, until he was there most of the night. Eclipse was either next to my chair or somewhere else close by watching me as always, but it seemed as though she was also carefully watching Mozart.

Before you say to yourself, "Wow, what a big deal. The dogs just changed their sleeping habits." Before you accuse me of making a big deal out of nothing there is one additional fact that I should let you know about. It certainly changed our thoughts on what was happening. Ready? A few weeks or so later Eclipse was dead. (Just writing that sentence has me tearing up, and it happened six months ago.

I bet you can guess our theory. Eclipse somehow knew that she was not going to be with us much longer, and that somebody had to take over her job of watching over me. This required a month or two of training her replacement. Namely Mozart. From that point on he slept by my side at all times. Yeah, I know. My wife and I are silly to think that this "Passing of the torch," was actually happening between the two dogs. Ridiculous to assign this kind of thinking ability to two canines, right? And your explanation is what, may I ask??

Beginning of the End

It was a Saturday night and everything was normal. The dogs ate their dinner with gusto, and went out around 7:30 as they always did. At 9:30 we always let them out for the final time. Eclipse didn't want to go out. This has happened before and you sometimes almost had to force her to go. We got her outside and all was fine. In they came and went to their positions. Mozart would always go into the dining room and Eclipse would sit by the sink in the kitchen. We would then give them a small biscuit treat, as we generally did when they came in. Training is very important, and as you can see they had us well trained.

Then, something happened that scared us both. Might not seem frightening to you, but to my wife and I there couldn't be anything more ominous. Eclipse took a piece of a small biscuit but didn't want the second one. For a dog that lived for food of any kind, this was not good. It never happened before. Right after her jaw cancer surgery she was eating ravenously, so for her not to accept the food that night was totally abnormal. I put a little bit of cream cheese on my finger which she accepted. No enthusiasm, just acceptance.

She laid down in the dining room in one of her positions to keep her eye on me. During the night I found her lying by the couch watching me. Not one of her usual spots. I went over and talked to her for a while. In the morning she was watching me while lying on the cool tiles by the front door. This was one of her favorite spots, since she liked cold places. My first thought was, "Back to normal, yes!"

She didn't get up. While Eclipse didn't seem in any distress or pain, even the breakfast ritual didn't move her from the tiles. No way this was possible. Something was obviously wrong. My sincere hope was that she had eaten something in the yard and got a little stomach upset. Then again, she could have eaten ten bad eggs, six poison mushrooms, gotten deadly sick, and would still be waiting by her food bowl! Not good at all. She was obviously going through something that I could in no way figure out.

Of course it was seven o'clock on a Sunday and my local vet was closed. So what did I do? I got right on the phone to Melanie, the head of the rescue group. This lady has as much dog medical knowledge as a whole pack of vets. I think I tried to explain what was going on, and got about three sentences into it when she said, "Sounds like the spleen." I was instructed to immediately get the dog to an emergency hospital that the group had used with success in the past. Melanie then said one thing that simply tore me apart. "If it is the spleen, they are going to tell you they can save your dog.....they can't." While she said it could be a urinary tract infection or something else, I had the feeling that she was saying this for my benefit, and to keep hope alive. She told me she would keep her phone with her at all times and I should call whenever we needed her.

Opening the front door near where Eclipse was laying, we coaxed her to come outside. She did, at a speed of a few feet per minute. I opened the hatch on the back of the car. Here was a dog, obviously in great distress and what does she do? She slowly struggles to take about a ten foot detour so she can urinate on the grass. In all the years we had her she had never had an accident of any kind in the house, and I guess she was not going to start now. When done, she slowly made her way to the car, looked up into it, and then looked at me as if to say, "I can't really make it up there."

We picked her up, and gently placed her in the vehicle, and off we went. It took twenty minutes or so to reach the emergency hospital, and I won't even attempt to relate my feelings during the drive. They ranged everywhere from hope to total despair. Upon arriving we had the staff come out and carry Eclipse inside. While we filled out the necessary paperwork she was taken in for a preliminary exam. The veterinarian came to see us and requested that we allow her to do an ultrasound. She could have asked me to donate a kidney to Eclipse and I would have been in the operating room in a split second. Are you kidding? I would have given her both if she had needed them.

Promise Kept

A little while later we were told that the spleen had been bleeding, and the tumor was large. She asked if we would like a chest x-ray which would have revealed if the cancer had spread to the lungs. We called Melanie. It is a veterinarian's job to do everything humanly possible to save an animal. I understand this. I also knew from my hospice experience that there are human doctors out there who will try, "one more thing, "even though it is obvious that the patient has no real chance of benefitting from it. There is also the possibility that the suggested treatments might make the remaining time even more uncomfortable.

Melanie talked to the vet for probably a half hour. I could catch some of the conversation. She basically said that Eclipse and I were very special to the rescue group and deserved to have the facts laid out for us. I was to find out later that when Melanie asked the vet what she would do if it was her dog (always a key question, but one that many will not answer), she had said, "I'd do everything possible) When Melanie asked how many she had saved that had this condition, the total figure could be counted on one hand. Apparently the rescue group, in all of their years had one dog successfully survive with this condition, and this dog's tumor of the spleen had been found almost by accident as part of an exam for something else. Luckily, after her talk with Melanie, the vet agreed to answer our questions bluntly. I inquired as to what the chances were that the spleen removal and subsequent treatment would be successful in Eclipse's case. Based upon her age etc., she was given about a five percent chance. A spleen that had ruptured would just about always mean that the cancer had already spread by way of the bloodstream. Therefore she would suffer from it somewhere else. Also, while I know now that the spleen removal surgery is pretty straight forward, subsequent weeks can be filled with a lot of problems for the dog. All in all, a bleeding spleen tumor is not exactly the diagnosis you want to hear.

We had always told Eclipse that we would never let anything hurt her, and this was a promise we now kept. In this case, not letting anything hurt her was going to hurt us as nothing ever had before. I asked the same question of this vet as I had asked when my previous golden retriever Shasta had liver cancer. "Is she is any physical pain at this time." When told that she wasn't, my response was simply, "And she won't be!" We knew really serious pain was about to begin and that it would last forever. My wife and I were the ones about to suffer the pain.

After letting the veterinarian know of our decision she left the room. A few minutes later we see her walking back down the hallway towards our room, with Eclipse simply walking by herself behind her. We were told that they put her on the floor and she simply followed the vet to our room. Actually I think it was the other way around. My thoughts flashed back to her initial jaw cancer surgery, when she took all those turns in the hallway to lead me back to the room we were spending the night in.

As Eclipse neared our room, the vet made a comment that was probably just interesting to her, but to me held great meaning. She said, "Look at the tail." It was wagging. I know…..big deal. Eclipse was not a tail wager. Strange in and of itself, but my mind flew back to when we had to put Shasta to sleep. There we were with her on the table, with the vet administering the drugs that would slowly ease her into a deep sleep, and then end her life, and her tail was wagging. For years I had always thought of writing a book of dog philosophy. The title was to simply be, "Die Wagging." It was to be about how dogs can teach us how to live….and to die.

The staff provided a blanket on the floor for Eclipse to lie on. Of course she walked by it and laid down against the wall on the cool tiles, as she always loved to do. My wife said she had a look on her face that said, "Hey guys, something's wrong with me." Not to say she looked worried or in pain, just trusting that her people would handle any situation.

Our words and actions are not as important as our emotions in communicating with a dog. I'm sure you have heard people say that their dog somehow knows when they are ill, when company is coming, and a whole lot of other situations. They have some ability to enter our hearts and souls and just figure out our moods, and feelings. Here we are on the floor with her for fifteen minutes or so telling her we love her, and that she is a good girl, etc., all the while trying to sound upbeat and normal without giving out any signals that anything was wrong. I hope dogs cannot see into us too deeply, because at that level my wife and I were ripped apart.

We were as ready as we ever going to be, and asked the vet to return. While hugging her and sharing our thoughts and love with her, the drugs were administered, and she silently left this world. I always think how we let dogs die with dignity, in a pain free way while being held by their loved ones, yet humans are many times not afforded this same option. People die all the time alone and in pain. I remember in an early Hospice class we were told that the movie depiction of the dying person, dying in their bed with a smile on their face, while surrounded by loved ones is rarely something rarely experienced in real life. All this is perhaps off the topic, but is on the other hand, something worthy of thought.

Going back out into the waiting room, one member of the staff said, "You seem to be taking it rather well." I just said, "Not really." Guess she wasn't that good at looking into people's hearts. Then again, she was not a dog, so I can't fault her.

The Funeral

All of our other dogs are buried in an animal cemetery. For those of you who have never seen one of these, you owe it to yourself to visit someday, particularly around the holidays. Around Christmas, many gravesites have toys, decorations, and small Christmas trees (some even lit using batteries). I always remember one summer visiting the cemetery where my parents are buried. All the grass was burned from the lack of rain. One or two gravesites had some wilted flowers, but other than that it was barren to say the least. Leaving there, we went to the animal cemetery. Beautifully green, neatly cut grass was being watered by a sprinkler system. Many graves had colorful flowers, etc. My wife and I attempted to purchase two larger size plots for our future use. Unfortunately the establishment has some discriminatory policy declaring that humans may not be buried there. How unfair.

After spending some time with Eclipse as she made the journey to the Rainbow Bridge, I called the pet cemetery to set up an appointment for a private cremation the following morning.

We drove home and told Mozart what had happened. Not sure if he quite understood. As I mentioned before, I sleep in a recliner in the living room. That night I did not have Eclipse at my side. I did however have Mozart there.....and my wife. She spent the night on the floor with him right by my chair. There are times when a family just must stay together.

Why no burial for Eclipse? Selfishness on my part I suppose. I wanted her with me even in death. Additionally, with my own weird disease that does not lend itself to a long life, the thought was even more on my mind, (although I am working quite hard to be the first survivor.....why not?) I always told my wife that Eclipse's ashes would be buried with me. Unfortunately not on the hill in the dog cemetery, but I guess you can't have everything. If, as you read this you are saying to yourself, "This guy is weird," let me inform you that this guy would certainly agree, as would most of those who knew him over the years. Remember however that being known as weird (Howierd by many) gives me a big leeway for behavior. When I do something unusual people just say, "Oh, that's just Howard." Let's you lead an interesting life!

The next morning we returned to the emergency hospital, and gently laid Eclipse in the back of the car for her final ride. Another tearjerker. We arrived at the cemetery and met the workers whom we knew from before. They were always supportive and understanding. Eclipse was placed in a viewing room and we spent some time with her. I won't get into the details, but let's just say every emotion of grief there is came to the surface. I then insisted that we stay with her while she was placed in the cremation oven. While most people would have skipped this part, my feeling was that she had never left my side and wouldn't under any circumstances. I wasn't about to leave her for even a minute at the end of her time on earth, regardless of the situation.

Might seem strange to think about a viewing room for an animal. Sometimes it's necessary. I remember when my brother King the basset hound died. Our family went to the pet cemetery for the burial. They asked if we wanted to see the dog, and we said yes. A minute later we came out of the viewing room and said, "That's not King." The attendant said they look different in death. Maybe so, but we doubted the change would be so dramatic as to make him appear to be a cat. A bit of a mix-up which they took care of right away. So viewing is necessary.☺

We received many, many sympathy cards. A human's family would be honored to receive so many! One message on our answering machine sort of said it all in terms of how loved she was by all. The message basically said, "I heard about Eclipse. I don't know what to say. I, I, don't know what to say. I feel so (followed by silence.)" Basically the message went on this way for some time. The caller was in such a state of sadness that words would not come out. Who was this person that couldn't express her emotions, and was at a loss for words? It was the grief counselor social worker for Hospice. Sort of puts the way everyone felt in perspective.

We left and returned a few hours later to pick up her ashes. They said we could come back another day, but there was no way I was leaving my baby there. We rode home in basically a state of shock.

Eclipse is now in an urn, inside of which, in addition to her ashes, is a picture of her, my wife, and myself. The urn is placed on a cabinet a few feet from my chair. In a way Eclipse is still watching me 24/7……and I am watching her.

The Rainbow Bridge

Just this side of heaven is a place called
Rainbow Bridge. When an animal dies that has
been especially close to someone here, that pet
goes to Rainbow Bridge. There are meadows and
hills for all of our special friends so they can run
and play together. There is plenty of food, water
and sunshine, and our friends are warm and
comfortable. All the animals who had been ill and
old are restored to health and vigor. Those who
were hurt or maimed are made whole and strong
again, just as we remember them in our dreams of
days and times gone by.

The animals are happy and content, except for one small thing; they each miss someone very special to them, who had to be left behind. They all run and play together, but the day comes when one suddenly stops and looks into the distance. His bright eyes are intent. His eager body quivers. Suddenly he begins to run from the group, flying over the green grass, his legs carrying him faster and faster. You have been spotted, and when you and your special friend finally meet, you cling together in joyous reunion, never to be parted again. The happy kisses rain upon your face; your hands again caress the beloved head, and you look once more into the trusting eyes of your pet, so long gone from your life but never absent from your heart.

Then you cross Rainbow Bridge, TOGETHER!!

Author unknown...

E

The other day I started some physical therapy for a back problem. My therapist asked a simple question with a complex answer. "What is that "E," he wondered? While giving some details of its origin, I basically told him that it is a philosophy of life.

A week after Eclipse's death a thought occurred to me. It should be obvious to everyone at this point that I would never forget my girl. It goes way beyond this however. In her nonverbal way, she imparted ideas on the correct way to live. To honor her memory, and have a physical, constant item with me at all times to look at when I needed inspiration, I purchase a tie tack letter "E," I wear it on my shirt all day, every day. When I was at the jeweler ordering it, I was given a couple of choices as to what it would be made of. Only one seemed appropriate.....PURE GOLD.

After reading the last couple of paragraphs, you probably have a good inkling that at this point I am going to spout off on exactly what this philosophy is all about. You're right. Its meaning is tremendously multifaceted to me, so I'll just go into some of the basics. Hopefully one or two of the thoughts will resonate with you, and just make good common sense. If not, remember in the preface, I clearly stated that I was writing this entire book for myself, so don't say I didn't warn you ☺

Eclipse lived each minute of her life never looking forward or backward. And she lived it well. We all could gain from getting in that grove. As they say, yesterday is only a dream, and tomorrow is only a vision, but today well lived makes every yesterday a dream of happiness, and every tomorrow a vision of hope. She really had this philosophy down to a "T".

She also set priorities, and there were only basically four of them. Of primary importance was being with the family. Then there was the concept of "doing good for others." After this came the ability to eat and poop. Actually Eclipse might have argued a bit here to get eating into position number one! I guess if we humans can say we possess these four things we should be pretty satisfied with the way our lives are going. Money, power, etc., are great I suppose, but without Eclipse's four priorities, all the rest are rather meaningless.

Make a difference. A simple statement, and a philosophy that Eclipse obviously lived each day.

Hey, if we don't share it, what good is it. We can always do something for someone. It doesn't have to be earth shattering either. A simple smile or word of reassurance can work wonders. You don't have to save the world. I'm always reminded of the story about the man on the beach who is throwing starfish that had been washed up on shore back into the sea. Another person comes by and says, "There are millions of them all along the beach. What possible difference can you make?" With this, the man picks up one more and throws it into the water, while saying, "Made a difference to that one." I can recall times when we would be in the hospital or nursing home and be told a patient hadn't communicated or spoken for weeks. In we would go and within minutes he or she would be talking to Eclipse. She made a difference just being there.

Do not love to be loved in return. Eclipse didn't expect to receive anything for the sharing of her love. It just came natural for her to love.

Don't "read into things." Sometimes we try to analyze things too much. Eclipse was, "just there." She saw a person, and she went over to them. She was offered love and she took it. I'm sure she didn't try to find the "true" reason that someone needed her to be there. She simply knew that she was needed.

Age is a number. Dogs don't know how young or old they are. They simply live. If they can't move due to some physical problem at age one, they don't. If they can run at fourteen, they do. Humans would be so bummed out by the first scenario, and elated at the second. Perhaps we should all try to learn to accept what is, and continue to "live," regardless of the circumstances. Dogs just "move on." Perhaps we should learn to do this also.

Show your true feelings and be yourself. It's all we really have. Eclipse simply went through life being Eclipse. She never tried to do something that was not in her nature, and certainly never tried to be just like some other dog that she had met. Sure worked out well for her and for everyone she came in contact with.

Dogs just, "move forward." They don't think about yesterday or tomorrow; or how fair or unfair life or a current situation is. They just treat every moment as the beginning of the rest of their lives. They deal with things as they are, not as they were or should be. Sometimes we are so busy planning our lives that we never get a chance to actually live them.

Never be dying. Can't avoid it, huh? Yes you can. Eclipse certainly did. While you can't avoid winding up dead someday, you can choose to "live to the fullest of your ability," until it arrives. I guess that's the," Die Wagging" philosophy.

I could probably go on and on, spouting the philosophy of the "E," but you get the point. There are many worthwhile lessons to be learned from our canine buddies. We just have to be open to adopting them into our lives. I have a feeling the world would be a much better place. So wag people, wag!!

Mozart's Surgery

This is not a chapter that I ever even remotely imagined would be in this book. It's certainly one I wish were not included.

Remember the chapter about Starbucks. I wrote that one in a local Starbucks where Eclipse and I would spend quite a few hours a week just chilling out. It was hard to actually write about it while sitting there sipping a coffee, while looking at the floor by my feet every few minutes at the empty space, which corresponded to the empty space in my heart and life. This chapter is also being written as events are currently taking place. Unfortunately, not good ones.

Once in a while my wife and I will spend a few days at a resort/casino in Connecticut. When my illness and chemo were going strong I could hardly walk from one place to another without getting weak and out of breath. One day we went to spend two nights at a casino where I could bring my oxygen, walker and scooter. For some reason I felt noticeably better during our time there. One theory is the controlled environment. Whatever the actual cause may be, the results continue, so we go there for a few days every two or three months. Maybe it's the electric energy given off by the slot machines. If it works it works, that's sort of the bottom line. We gamble very little. Let's put it this way, I actually frequent a bank of 1/4 cent slot machines. Ok, at times I even go for a whole penny! We'll never walk away big winners, and only hope to leave as little losers.

When we go away anywhere, we have the vice president of the rescue group come to our home to watch the dogs,....now dog. She spends the day and overnight here, and I always know that we need not worry for an instant. She always treats them wonderfully, and cares for them as if they were her own.

A week or two ago, after we returned from one of our outings, she mentioned that Mozart had a tick or something by his mouth. She noticed it just before leaving on the last day, and felt we would be better able to remove it when we got home. My wife found it, and decided to remove whatever it was the next morning. It was gone. Or so she thought. Not being able to find it we assumed it was something that got stuck on there and had since fallen off. Mozart always gets his flea and tick treatment each month, so it was logical to assume that if it was a tick, it would not be feeling so good, and would certainly die and fall off. A couple more days of looking, and nothing. Then for some reason my wife notices it again. While it still might have been a tick, a trip to the vet was indicated. He was about due anyway to pay a friendly visit, so it was no big deal. As it turned out, a big deal was exactly what it turned out to be.

The next morning we arrived for his visit. He and Eclipse always loved going to the vet. She would feed them biscuits during the exams, which resulted in them absolutely loving to go there. For a golden retriever food is where it's at. Their attitude is basically, "Do what you want to me, just keep those treats coming." When a rectal temperature is required, the rule is simple. The vet puts something in one end, while I would put some treats in the other. To the dogs, this balanced things out nicely.

She saw the thing under his mouth, which was probably a mole or something. Its darkened color concerned her a bit, so she felt it would be good to remove it. Upon further exam it was discovered that one of his fatty growths on his back leg was harder than it should be, and removing and biopsying it, would also be a good idea. After some added discussion, the veterinarian mentioned that while it certainly wasn't necessary, she could do a set of body x-rays while he was under anesthetic. An older dog and anesthesia do not mix too well, so we figured that while he was "out" anyway, we might as well have it done. We even decided to have his teeth cleaned up and the tartar removed. Not a scenario we pictured a few days before, but certainly within the realm of acceptability. He was to have everything done the following day.

I'm certain Mozart hated the concept of surgery with a passion. After all he had to do without food in the morning. What could be worse than this? We tried to get up later than usual, and altered our normal routine, to keep him off balance a bit in the morning. It's seemed to work, but I'm sure some part of him was saying, "Somehow I do not remember eating today." Around nine in the morning we headed up to the veterinary hospital.

As those of you who have dogs know, there's hardly a stranger feeling than returning to a home and not being greeted at the door, or at least seeing your friend lying around somewhere. The day of the surgery we felt like something was "just not right," whenever we entered the house. It's funny how we complain about them stopping us from just going where we want, for as long as we want, getting fur on the floor, and a bunch of other annoying stuff. I suppose the only thing worse is not having them around annoying us.

We were concerned during the day. With possible problems for him on the horizon, and just having lost Eclipse a few months before, I can't say we had very positive thoughts about the day's outcome. How "ungolden," like of us. There was never a question that we would do whatever was needed to help the boy. Decisions would be made at all times based on the benefits to him, and his quality of life, not ours.

Seven thirty that evening we went up to get him. Going into the back surgical area with the doctor, we certainly expected to see a drugged up animal just about recovering from surgery, and all the anesthesia and pain killers involved. Here he was on the floor just hanging out with one of the vet techs. When we came in with the veterinarian, he gets up and walks over. Seemed pretty normal to me. What does he do when he sees this person who just cut him up? Naturally he tries to stick his head in her pocket to see if she has any cookies in there. Yes, he was back to normal. Canines just "move on," and simply do not dwell on the past or the future. Only the present has true meaning, and a pocket full of biscuits certainly classifies as having true meaning! She said that he had been eating them out of house and home.

Now, for the results of the surgery. The growth by the mouth as well as the large back leg lump, and a small eye growth were all removed. She tried to get all the surrounding tissues so that the areas would have a "clean margin," and in that way, hopefully any troublesome cells would have been removed, and spreading of whatever these things were would be lessened, or hopefully eliminated. With stitches everywhere, he looked a bit like Frankendog, particularly since a golden is covered with tons of fun, and now he had large areas that had been shaved. Someone, somewhere, could probably make a few dollars selling "fur wigs," for dogs. I realize that is a ridiculous idea that could only appeal to people who are a little bit off the deep end. Of course most dog owners have gone over the edge a long time ago, so I'll have to see if Amazon.com sells this item.

X-Rays and Ultrasounds

Time to see the x-rays. As I mentioned we had them done even though they were not needed, since he was going to be anesthetized anyway. The vet said they looked pretty good, and showed us a nice shot of the lungs which were fine. All good news......so far. Putting up another x-ray, she says, "If you look here." What's right in front of me is the one part of the body that I really didn't want to see with some shadowing on it.

Yes, the spleen! One of the top golden retriever areas of cancer, and the condition that proved fatal for Eclipse. There were basically three possibilities. The x-ray might not be showing a tumor after all (a relatively small possibility given the breed and age). If it was a tumor it could be either benign or malignant. Naturally either of the second possibilities would require removal of the spleen, and quickly. These things rupture fast, and once they do there is just about no chance of saving the animal. Serious surgery followed by chemotherapy can keep the dog alive for a limited time, but the cancer has almost certainly spread and will shortly appear somewhere else. Some might have other feelings in the matter, but the general agreement among members of the rescue group is that treating a ruptured tumor of the spleen is not a smart thing to do. I'm sure there are dogs out there that lived fairly good lives for a few more months, but for each of these there were many who spent the rest of their extremely shortened lives (assuming they even survived the surgery) with discomfort, etc.

While we would wish to keep him around for as long as possible, as soon as it becomes obvious that to do so only fulfills our needs and not his, it is time to lovingly assist him in his exit from this life. A day or so later a specialist would be coming to our vet's office to do an ultrasound. This would be the definitive test to see what we were dealing with.

Dropping Mozart off at the office at nine on Monday morning, we knew we would be returning around three that afternoon to find out the results. To be honest with you, good news was not exactly high on our list of expectations.

Three o'clock. We enter the veterinary hospital and receive the results. In the spleen there were only some nodules that are quite common to a dog of Mozart's age, and should not present any problems. They certainly would not require surgery. Additional ultrasound was also performed and no evidence of other developing problems was seen. His bladder was a little thickened, and urine showed some increase in white cells which could just be due to an infection.

Home we went with some added antibiotics, and smiles on our faces. It was still hard to fathom that the test results were negative. While we had to wait for the other biopsies to come back, compared to the possible spleen cancer, at least these would probably be treatable.

The following day result number one came in negative for the growth under the chin. A day later negative findings arrived for the large growth that had been removed from his hind leg. Never would have dreamed everything would have worked out so well.

As I write this paragraph Mozart is lying next to me with his pirate hat on. Actually it's one of those cone things to prevent the animal from getting at stitches, etc. Some dogs cannot stand the cones, but he actually likes to put it on, since for some reason when your head goes through it, there is a piece of kibble on the other side. Must be some kind of magic! He takes his pills easily by just having them in his bowl with his meals. I just had a tooth extraction and was on the antibiotic Amoxicillin, which is one of the drugs he takes, so we just have antibiotic parties. I think my wife may be jealous.

Biopsies with negative results, along with good ultrasound results. Doesn't get much better than that for an almost twelve year old golden retriever. Of course all the stitches, and everything else, resulted in quite a few return trips to the animal hospital. Mozart is ecstatic! More visits equals more treats. A formula which works quite well for him.

Since Eclipse's death I have gotten to know Mozart well. As I mentioned before, when my girl was around she would put herself between me and him. Now that it was just he and I, we really bonded. Took awhile though. Somewhere on the order of two hours.

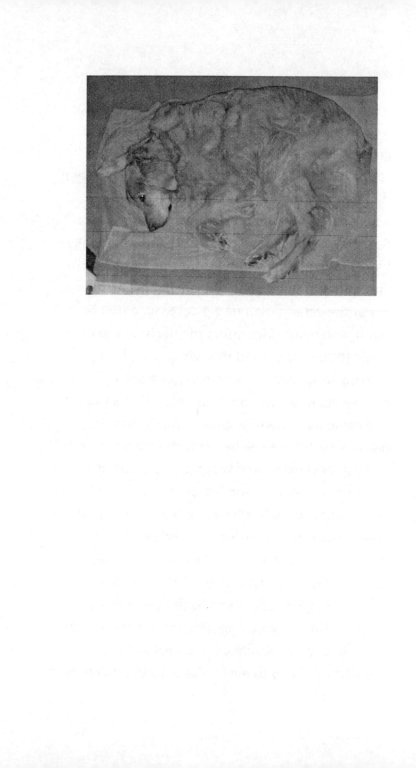

Here We Go Again

A couple of months ago Mozart had gotten a clean bill of health. A few weeks back a fast growing lump was discovered. Many tests, and specialist vet visits later, the conclusion was drawn that he had a relatively rapid growing cancer, where surgery would not benefit him in the long run. We watched him like a hawk, and would take him to the vet each week. As long as his quality of life continues to be good, we are happy. As soon as either the veterinarian or we determine that he is having too much discomfort the decision will be made to send him on to the rainbow bridge to be with his sister. Again, the beauty of a dog is that he or she lives in the moment, adapts to the situation, and never ever has thoughts of death. I know when his time comes, he will be up at the animal hospital looking for cookies, and wagging his tail. While this will be a simpler decision for us to make than it was with Eclipse, we will still have a few doubts as to whether our decision is correct. While I know we did the right thing letting Eclipse leave this world, I still have "what if," thoughts. What if I had the spleen removed? Could she have lived a little bit longer, while still enjoying life? For me, having her for an hour more would be wonderful. Those of you who have had to euthanize a dog, certainly can relate. We just hope we made the right decision. With Mozart it is still going to tear us apart! His final resting place will be in an urn right next to his sister, where we can all continue to keep an eye on each other.

Eclipse and Mozart – Together Again

When I wrote the last chapter, Mozart was still with us. Now he is not.

A week or so after writing the last chapter our local veterinarian noted that his gums were getting a bit paler, and there was some bruising, which probably indicated internal bleeding.

We took him back a few days ago, and the conditions were getting worse. We also noticed him slowing down more at home, but with increased medication, I don't think he was in any real pain. It was a Monday, and we decided to bring him back and send him on his journey to the Rainbow Bridge to be with his sister on Thursday. On Monday through Wednesday we treated him extra special (as if that's possible ☺) We spent a large portion of those days in the car, which was always a favorite activity of his.

Thursday arrived. Not a fun day for us, but I have a feeling it was one of his favorites. The day was composed of perpetual homemade burritos, ham, hot dogs, biscuits, special doggie treats, and basically anything else we could give him, including his favorite, tennis balls. From a dog that didn't get "people food, "he instantly went to one that gets to eat the entire contents of the refrigerator.

Just before five in the evening we took him for the last car ride in this life. We rode to the water with him and parked for a bit. Then it was on to the vet.

Try to picture him on the table eating handfuls of the biscuits they had ready for him. He was inhaling them, and then two seconds later he was gone. Not a bad way for an animal to go, I suppose. Heck, not a bad way for a human to go either; eating tons of treats and not knowing life was to end. And yes, all the while his TAIL WAS WAGGING!

The vet had a box of tissues ready for us. I remember my only comment was, "You must be very optImistic to only have one box for us. " We easily emptied it. We spend some time in the room with our boy, knowing that he was now with his sister.

That evening we took six of his human friends out to dinner, to celebrate his life. While he would have liked the concept, I can't get around the fact that he would have enjoyed the food even more. That's my boy!

The next morning we picked him up for his final ride for a private cremation. Boy, did that bring back memories of Eclipse's cremation several months before. The people at the animal rescue organization that do the cremations are wonderful. They treat the people and the dog with respect. After spending some time in the viewing room with Mozart, it was time for us to go. We returned a few hours later to get him, and he now has his place at home right next to his sister, and across from my chair.

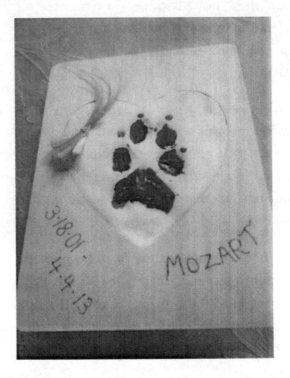

Sort of Sums It Up

I lied. I remember writing several weeks ago that when the decision was made to send Mozart on his way, that it would be easier than it had been with Eclipse. It wasn't! The decision to send Eclipse to the bridge had to be made instantly, while his was well thought out. Let me tell you, it tore us up just as much. I guess that the saying is true; grief is the price we pay for love.

The best way to explain the way my wife and I feel, can best be summed up by Dr.Seuss who said, "Don't cry because it's over, smile because it happened". At this point, we certainly do smile because it happened. Our lives with Eclipse and Mozart gave us the most pleasurable times. That part of the quote we are good with, and there are many smiles of memory. However, the "Don't cry," part refuses to show itself to this day. Just proves how wonderful these beings are!

While the loss of both of our friends is obviously devastating, it's only the second worst type of loss. The worst would have been the loss of never having had the honor of sharing our lives with them.

I'm sure we'll see our special friends again. If you have lost a beloved pet, I'm sure you will too. As the song says, "A breath away's not far from where you are."

Not Really the End

End of the book, but not the end of the story. Writing it certainly was therapeutic for me. My hope is that is brought a little joy and stirred some thinking in the people who have read it. If it raised a few dollars for golden retriever rescue, that also would make the whole project even more worthwhile. Positive reviews at Amazon.com are always appreciated. Might mean more sales which equals more funds for the Goldens.

I urge everyone, that whenever possible, to live a little more like a golden retriever, minus the shedding of course, since this could make you a bit unpopular.

Have a golden day, and never NEVER MISS A GOLDEN OPPORTUNITY!

<u>Long Island Golden Retriever Rescue</u>

P.O.Box 566

Plainview, NY 11803

516-578-3803 (Rescue Phone)   516-932-0017 (Fax)

LIGRR.ORG

LIGRR is a 501 (C)(3) Non-profit. Therefore all donations are totally tax deductable.

Donations can be sent to the P.O.Box or use PayPal.   The dogs say, "Thanks."

9.99

CPSIA information can be obtained at www.ICGtesting.com
Printed in the USA
LVOW13s1421100814

398432LV00001B/39/P